Debbi

Be Inspired
Be Inspired

Psalm 82:3

Pieces

of

My

Heart

Elizabeth Hunter Molina

Scripture quotations marked NASB are taken from the New American Standard Bible ® (NASB), Copyright © 1960, 1962, 1963, 1968, 1971, 1972, 1973, 1975, 1977, 1995 by the Lockman Foundation. Used by permission. www.Lockman.org

Scripture quotations marked NIV are taken from the Holy Bible, *New International Version,* ® *NIV.*® Copyright © 1973, 1987, 1984, 2011 by Biblica, Inc. ® Used by permission. All rights reserved worldwide.

The views presented in the text are the sole opinions of the author unless otherwise stated.

Some names have been changed in order to maintain confidentiality.

ISBN-13: 9781545531921

ISBN-10: 1545531927

Pieces of My Heart. Copyright © 2018 Elizabeth Hunter Molina.

Cover design by Lianne Frame.

Cover photo © Shandi Noakes Photography.

Printed in the United States of America

Dedicated to my children -

Jordan, Grant, Hope, and Laura.

You are the pieces of my heart.

CONTENTS

	Acknowledgments	vii
	Foreword	ix
	Introduction	xi
1	First Comes Love	1
2	Then Comes Marriage	7
3	Roller Coaster	15
4	Sign Me Up!	21
5	Matched!	29
6	Meeting Gualège	35
7	The Best Gift	51
8	Summer Lovin'	59
9	I'll Be Back	73
10	Bittersweet	79
11	The Firsts	89
12	Third-World Kids in the First World	105
13	A Baby Sister	129
14	Starting over Again	139
15	Broken Heart	153

16	The Call	159
17	Fake It 'til You Make It	169
18	Love Story Complete	177
	Afterword	187
	Notes	191
	Organizations/Resources	197

Acknowledgements

Special thanks to...

My husband, Mario, who has always loved the kids and I (and all our pets) well.

My dear friend, Dianna, who painstakingly read through the very first draft.

My sister, Amy, for showing me my tenderhearted side.

Friends, Joanna and Kim, for being test-readers and plowing all the way through the first draft when it was still pretty bad.

Dr. Stacey Newman for lending your medical expertise in infectious diseases. You make me sound like I know what I am talking about.

Craig Juntunen, for clarifying my description of your very informative film, *Stuck*.

Michelle Beard, for going through the text, line by line, not holding back. Your constructive criticism saved me some embarrassment.

Debbie Barber you are gifted with the ability to see the whole story before it is complete, what is missing, where the gaps are, and what needs to be said to make it an infinitely better story.

Lianne Frame, your artistic eye for the front and back cover design is remarkable.

Debbie Sourgen, you have a true servant's heart. By going through the text numerous times with a fine-toothed comb to catch every grammatical error (and there were many), you have made me look like a very good writer.

My first friend for life, Shelby, this labor of love that you helped birth has come to fruition only because, in true friend fashion, you have stuck by me through it all from start to finish.

Elizabeth Molina

Foreword

We had just finished our small group Bible study and, as we so often did, we invited the children to come in from the other room to join us for prayer time. They came running into our living room, ready to pray and then enjoy some dessert. I remember that this night dessert would be less important and that our prayer time would take on new meaning. We were accepting prayer requests and, as if they had planned it, Jordan and Grant both asked us to pray for their friends and family in Haiti as they had just suffered a devastating earthquake.

That was a special night for everyone in the group. You see, we learned more about Haiti but we also got a glimpse into the heart of two young boys. Two boys that were learning a new language, a new culture, and meeting new friends. We were also learning about adoption and the journey a family must take to bring adoptive children into their home.

The story of adoption as experienced by the Molina family is an incredible journey of persistence, compassion, and, of course, the blessings of a God that loves them very much. I have enjoyed the privilege of walking with them through many of the difficult steps of foreign and domestic adoption. I have prayed with them when everything was going well and when the process was difficult. I was honored to watch them welcome these scared, uncertain, but very excited children into their family.

I am so grateful that my friend Elizabeth has written the book you hold in your hands. I want many more people to hear this story, to be amazed at God's love displayed in the process of adoption, and to consider adopting children themselves. In these pages, you will not only encounter one family's story of adoption but you will also experience the amazing grace of our loving heavenly Father.

We eventually did make it to the dessert table and guess who was at the front of the line? Two hungry young boys, ready to eat. Read on and enjoy.

Mike Newman
Senior Pastor
LifeWay Baptist Church,
Ventura, CA

Introduction

Many people have asked me about our adoption story. I often find myself grappling over what words to use and which details to share, knowing that they probably have time only for the "nut-shell" version. I don't want to simplify the work God did in our family by chopping it down to a 20-second sound bite to satisfy a curiosity. It is a story worth its weight in gold only because of who its true Author is. So I thank you in advance for being willing to sit and read our whole story.

> *We long to live a God-sized story, but all great stories begin with love.*[1]

I grew up in a lower socioeconomic neighborhood, on the "other side of the tracks." Many Saturday mornings I would sit on the front porch of our government-assisted housing, known as The Projects, and wonder about my life. I would daydream about all the great and wonderful things I would do when I finally got out of there. I imagined all the things that I would do to make a name for myself. As I grew up and carved a path in the world, I realized that it wasn't me determining my steps. Proverbs 16:9 says, "The mind of man plans his way, but the Lord directs his steps" (NASB). There was this incredibly powerful and loving God who was guiding me through life. I could choose to do things my own way or follow His direction, in faith. As an adult, my thoughts once again turned to this idea of doing something God-sized. I hadn't really ever seen our adoption story as this great thing that we did. It was simply our way of building our family. But in crediting the true Author, I realize it really is something wonderfully God-sized.

> *...measure your life by how well you have loved. In the moment that you love well, you are the most like Jesus.*[2]

My husband had a menagerie of pets when we first met. Each time I was over to his apartment it seemed like a new pet would emerge, literally out of the woodwork! One day a ball python popped its head out of a kitchen drawer; another day a tortoise made its way out of a closet it had been hibernating in. While it was endearing at first, I couldn't understand why he always wanted more animals! One day he rescued a baby squirrel that accidentally entered our garage and couldn't find its way out. Another time he helped a baby crow that had fallen out of a tree in our yard. On a walk one afternoon he shooed away crows picking at a baby jackrabbit in the orchard by our house. He brought it home to nurse it back to health. It seemed the local bulldog rescue had him on speed-dial!

I began to notice a pattern. And so I slowly began to understand his heart...and the heart of God. When we decided to try out foster-adopt, I saw it as a way to add to our family while he saw it, additionally, as an opportunity to love another that needed help when they were most vulnerable. We have loved when it has not been the easy choice but, in those moments, we were loving well. Our family was built while experiencing many of the same joys of biological families, but enduring the added struggles of adoptive families. Our non-traditional family is rooted in the love that Christ calls every believer to demonstrate. The kind of love that costs the heart much.

God is the author of all great love stories.[3]

As I read these profound words, I felt it was God impressing upon my heart to write our family story. When I was asked to speak for the second time at Adoption Story Night, I intended to ask my dear friend Shelby to listen to me speak that night to see if she would be willing to help me improve my presentation or even help me write our family story. If for no one else, then for my children. Adopted children want and need to know how they came to be part of the family. After the night was over, I accompanied Shelby to her car and she said, "I would really love to help you polish up your presentation or even get it on paper if you have some time." I was ecstatic! You see, I hadn't had the time to contact Shelby that day. But God, in His sovereignty, had gone before us and guided our steps which led to this collaborative work.

My husband will say that I start a million different projects and never have the time to finish one. I know this to be true about myself and so I admitted this to the Lord when I embarked on this journey of writing our story. He directed my friend to guide me through it and to hold my hand each step of the way to help me stay on track. As I sat each day at the computer, I asked the Lord for wisdom and to give me the words to write. On my own I would not have a story to tell. He is the Author of this great love story, this family.

Love begins with a choice and a commitment; in the end, love is a legacy that will be remembered forever.[4]

Soon after my husband and I were married, we assumed we would have a family the way the majority of the world did—naturally—but God's plan was different. His plan for our family was bigger and better than we could have ever imagined. It was heartbreaking to go through the trials of infertility, the long wait for international adoptions to be finalized, the struggles of letting go of love while fostering, and then staying the path that led to our forever daughters. Hardly does He share with us beforehand the road down which He will lead us, because we may decide not to go. We stepped out in faith on a journey to build our family, then trusted Him to be faithful each step of the way.

In her book, *Own your Life*, Sally Clarkson challenged me, the reader, to begin to think about what legacy I would leave for my children. We chose to adopt our children and our hearts are fully invested in loving them through to the end. My prayer is that through this book, God and our children will see that we loved well. You see, our story is one of love—love initiated, constructed, and sustained by God. He brought us together like the pieces of a puzzle and then wove our hearts to create our family, our legacy of love.

…

Each day my son Grant writes about what he read in his Bible that morning. When he hands it to me, he declares in his most charming voice, "That's a piece of my heart, Mama." He has put his all into it, trusting that not only will I be pleased with his effort but that God will also be pleased with his heart. If you are exploring adoption, are curious about adoptive families or how you can help them on their journey, or just want to read a God-sized story that warms your heart, then dive into this journey with me—it's a piece of my heart.

Loving and trusting God,
Elizabeth

Elizabeth Molina

1
First Comes Love...

"Come to Thomas's football game on Saturday morning; his Big Brother is coming," my sister said. She had been a single mom for a while and her oldest son was giving her a run for her money, like most kids do when hormones start kicking in full throttle. So she signed him up for the Big Brothers program in the hopes of providing him with a positive male role model. I think I was invited to the game to check out more than just my nephew's athletic skills!

I showed up to the game as promised and so did the Big Brother. I think my sister was hoping I would hit it off with this guy right away. She probably envisioned us having a conversation that lasted the duration of the game and then walking off together hand-in-hand. We spoke for all of two seconds. In fact I think we just said,

"Hi," and then, after a brief conversation with my sister, I had to leave before the game even started. While I was intrigued, I had a previous commitment.

Being pretty attached to my nephew and the free meals served at his house, I spent lots of time over there. It was not surprising that I happened to be there another time his Big Brother, Mario, was also there. My sister quickly reminded him as she pushed me into his space, "You remember my sister Liz?"

After a challenge to a game of chess, a run on the beach, and breakfast with him and the nephew, things were definitely starting to heat up. We finally planned an official date for the evening of Christmas Day. When the day arrived, I met up with him at my sister's house, of course. It probably wasn't his idea of a first date, especially since my nieces and nephews had us practically married before we got out the door. One of them had even checked some program on the computer to see if we were compatible based on our birthdays!

We hung out a few more times. It wasn't long before I was hooked on this guy. He was adorably awkward and nerdy, but at the same time so full of confidence. Everything about this guy was intriguing. The fact that he ironed every piece of clothing right down to his socks and underwear was entertaining!

In those first few months as I got to know him better, I noticed he had an unusual amount of pets for a bachelor. It should have been a warning sign, but it was endearing at first. I had seen a hamster and a tank with piranhas. Then one day I witnessed a tortoise, incidentally named Rocket, crossing his 8-by-12-foot studio apartment. I was hoping it would reach the lettuce he had set out before it wilted. The biggest surprise was a 3-foot ball python! I met it accidentally as I reached for a fork—it happened to be napping in his kitchen drawer!

This menagerie of animals was okay with me as long as I didn't have to live with them. I hadn't grown up with animals and the only pets I had as an adult were two cats that my coworker suggested I get "to help you develop a more sensitive side, Elizabeth." This was as a result of a class pet in our shared Kindergarten classroom that had failed to thrive. While my coworker was sad and sympathetic to the poor animal's plight, I thought it was time to put it out of its misery. She was mortified at my lack of sensitivity and marched me over to her friend's house to pick out two kittens. Day one of sensitivity training involved defleaing them.

I ended up giving the cats away after about six months because they were too much work. It was about that time I started dating Mario, who must have thought I was feeling bad about getting rid of them. One day he brought me an orphan kitty he had rescued from his workplace. He even agreed to keep and take care of it for me despite the fact that he was allergic to cats! I could visit and play with the kitten when I was at his house. This arrangement worked for me.

One of the things that initially struck me as most

interesting about Mario was that he didn't talk a whole lot. At first I thought he was either really shy or didn't know how to converse with women. However, it could have been that I didn't ever give him a chance to get a word in edgewise. At times, I thought maybe he was being antisocial. But as I got to know him more, I realized that he is just the reserved type. It didn't matter. It was too late. I had fallen for him.

I had been regularly dating Mario for a period of about five or six months. I was starting to appreciate what made him different from other guys. There was something special about this man, and I wanted to sort out my feelings and reflect on the relationship without being influenced by the physical attraction. I thought maybe I needed a break. He wasn't thrilled about the whole "taking a break" idea, but agreed to it. I thought maybe this guy could be the one for me, but I wasn't sure. I spent a good portion of that summer in prayer searching for God's purpose in our relationship.

Through the summer we saw each other from time to time. Shortly before the school year started, I took a trip to Hawaii. I was contemplating moving back there, and wanted to explore my work options. I had originally moved to Hawaii in the early part of 1991, attended college, and graduated from the University of Hawaii, Manoa. I loved the island lifestyle. While living on Oahu, I had become a Christian. A dear friend led me to the Lord, discipled me, and became my lifelong mentor. I was homesick for Hawaii but I had fallen in love with Mario and was now feeling torn. I wasn't sure where the relationship with Mario was going either. At 27 years old, marriage was high on my list of things I wanted to do before I turned 30. Having kids was right up there, too.

Elizabeth Molina

2
Then Comes Marriage...

After I returned from Hawaii, Mario and I planned a short trip up to Northern California to visit a good friend of mine. I had worked with her while in college in Hawaii. Even though she was raising three kids and attending college full time, she always welcomed me and let me crash on her sofa. Eight hours on the road made for a whole lot of time for Mario and I to talk. I was still attracted to Mario, but I was also starting to see him as a friend.

The drive back home was even more interesting. Up to this point in time, he had been attending church with me but I was unsure of his Christian status. This had always been a deal-breaker for me in the past. So when the topic of conversation in the car turned to the possibility of us dating again, I set some stipulations:

(1) we would attend church together on a regular basis, (2) we would date with long-term intentions, and (3) we would abstain from premarital sex. Surprisingly, he agreed to all of it!

That trip was a turning point in our relationship and shortly afterward it seemed as though things moved along quickly. Since our status had returned to "dating," we spent more time together getting to know each other better. We went to church on Sundays, even when he was coming off a night shift and could hardly keep his eyes open.

One night, while hanging out, the conversation suddenly got serious. I mentioned to him that I had looked for work during my visit to Hawaii and that I was considering sending out my resume. Although we were more intentional in our relationship, I was still a little unsure if it was me trying to make things happen or God leading. I don't know for sure how premeditated his words were but Mario asked what would keep me from moving back to Hawaii. Soon we were talking about going ring shopping. I never gave moving back to Hawaii another thought!

We spent the next six months planning our wedding, spending time with each other, and attending premarital counseling. That was eye opening! I think I realized then that neither one of us was very good at communicating and that if we didn't learn to, it could very possibly be a disastrous match. Mario was not a big talker and I was not a very good listener, at least not to the voices outside my head.

Possibly one of the best things in premarital counseling was when the pastor told us to bring a list of our absolutes—the big things that we absolutely would not change our minds about. Then, if the other could accept those things we could move forward or try to come to an acceptable compromise. One of my absolutes had to do with our kids' education (the ones we didn't even have yet). I reserved the right to either enroll them in private school or homeschool them. Mario has not always understood my reasoning for private education or homeschool, but he has honored his promise to abide by my absolutes. He would absolutely not give up his job. At the time, I felt confident that I could live with that. While being the wife of a police officer has its perks, it is not easy. The hours, the mandatory overtime, the daily risk of life, the burden of tension and stress they carry, the distrust and dislike of cops by many people, all make me a nervous wreck and on edge every time he leaves for work.

On a scorching hot day in April 2012, on the first hole of the Soule Park Golf Course in Ojai, we were married. We celebrated with our family and close friends. The next morning we headed off on our honeymoon. As if my falling asleep early on our wedding night was not bad enough, the next seven days of my being seasick and drugged up on Dramamine had to be a huge letdown for the poor guy. The all-night pizza bar must have made up for it though, because that is all he remembers of the 6-night, 7-day cruise to Baja. There are pictures to prove that I was there walking around, but my biggest memory is feeling sick or sleepy most of that time. Fortunately, we had a lifetime ahead of us to create memories together.

    I had read that the first year of marriage would be the hardest. It was true! The communication issue affected all aspects of our life. I was known for putting my foot in my mouth and immediately trying to repair the damage before I even got the last word out. I couldn't always tell if Mario was joking or serious or a little of both. The other area of difficulty in our marriage was finances. Being a control freak by nature, I felt like I needed to know exactly how every penny was being spent. When I finally gave up trying to control it and just handed over my paycheck, I realized how much easier life was. Finally trusting him to provide and to handle all the financial responsibilities gave me a sense of freedom. This has had an overwhelmingly positive impact on both the financial concerns and our ability to communicate about how our money is spent. Mario ultimately makes the final decisions and willingly bears the responsibility of those decisions.

    That first year wasn't all difficult, though. We would make up silly games to play with each other, try to outdo the other in gift giving and planning crazy adventures, all without spending a penny... just for the challenge. All the while we were learning to invest time in our relationship.

Most probably the sweetest thing we did for each other was write poems for Valentine's Day. We agreed about a month before the high pressure holiday that we weren't going to purchase gifts for each other that year. The poem was to be our gift. My sweet husband doesn't show his sensitive side very often (other than to animals) but he blew me away with the time and effort he put into his poem. He even printed it on fancy paper and framed it. I wish this story ended with me reciprocating like we agreed, but it doesn't. I completely forgot! I attempted to write a poem on a piece of paper before leaving work that day. In a panic I scribbled, "Roses are red, violets are blue, your tush is cute and so are you." Needless to say, it was a complete flop.

Years later, I wanted to redeem myself by writing him an actual poem for another Valentine's Day. The most sentimental thing I had ever given him were the words, "All My Love, All My Life" engraved on the inside of his wedding band. Based on this thought with which I entered our marriage, I wrote a poem describing all that he means to me. We weren't hoping to, nor did we win any literature awards, but we won each other's hearts on those Valentine's Days.

After the wedding, we had moved all of my furniture into storage and were living in his rental apartment. Instead of a kitchen table he had a weight bench, instead of a sofa he had a foam futon, and instead of a coffee table he had a trunk. It was screaming *bachelor pad* and I was ready for a nest. I decided that we should find something a little more grown up. And so began the process of making our first purchase. It almost didn't happen though.

As we walked into the loan office to get preapproved for a home loan (per the advice of the realtor), I was thinking about how quickly the pieces of life were coming together. It felt like I had waited forever. "I'm sorry, there seems to be a problem with your credit history," the loan officer said. And just like that my grand hopes of realizing another part of the dream came to a screeching halt, like the needle suddenly being ripped off the 33 record on a turntable. *"What?!"* I thought, as my head swung around with an accusing look straight at my new husband. Poor guy, he didn't even know what hit him! He had no idea what she was talking about and offered no words to defend himself. He managed to cough up a sketchy explanation about some beeper bill that may have gone unpaid back in the '80s.

As it turned out, my brother-in-law and his wife had their credit history mixed in with ours and vice versa. We were able to figure it all out once we saw the credit reports. These agencies assumed that my husband, Mario, and his brother, Manny, were one and the same person with an alias–and probably two very high maintenance wives!

We eventually did get preapproved and we bought

a two-bedroom condo in a nice little complex. We had many opportunities to work on our communication skills while turning it into our home. The ball python came with us as well as my cat and his piranhas. The fish tank was banished to the garage, the cat became an outdoor kitty, and Quentin, the snake, had to return to a confined lifestyle. He didn't last too much longer after that—he seemed depressed being stuck in a glass box all day.

While I thought it was perhaps time for us to start a family, my husband thought we should get a dog. So T-Bone, our beloved bulldog, came into the picture. Although I have never been a fan of living with animals, I did love having a cute little puppy. It was a lot of work! At least, I thought that until our kids came along. About a year later we added another bulldog to our pack, and then I thought it must be time to start having real kids.

Elizabeth Molina

3
Roller Coaster

Mario had told me that he wanted to wait at least four years before starting a family. I negotiated that down to two years and we got started. When I didn't get pregnant right away, I found justification in starting earlier. I hadn't imagined it would be so hard, though. It seemed like so many women were getting pregnant left and right without even trying! Every time I heard about another one, I would get frustrated. Okay, so maybe I wasn't a spring chicken, but I was only 30 or 31 years old. My doctor suggested I start on a drug called Clomiphene (Clomid) which can be a first step for treating unexplained infertility. Clomid is a hormone that stimulates ovulation in a normal cycle. After a few rounds of this with no results, following the advice of our doctors, we decided both of us would get tested.

The test results didn't show either one of us had any signs of being infertile. My eggs were dropping and his guys were swimming. I couldn't imagine it even being a problem in my family, what with all the grandkids and great-grandkids my mother already had.

    A friend recommended asking my gynecologist about having a hysterosalpingogram done. In this procedure, dye is injected into the uterus via a thin tube which is inserted through the vagina and cervix. The dye flows through the uterus and fallopian tubes. Finally it spills into the abdominal cavity. Pictures are taken with an x-ray. This shows if there are any obstructions or abnormalities. If the fallopian tubes are blocked then the dye will not spill into the abdominal cavity. The dye itself can potentially clear minor blockages. The results showed clear and no blockage in my tubes or any notable problems in my uterus. My friend had gotten pregnant with her first child right after she had that test done. Naturally, I thought the same thing would happen for me. It didn't.

    After months of trying, I did finally get pregnant. From the start it wasn't quite right. I knew I was late on my menstrual cycle but a home pregnancy test wasn't showing positive. Finally, we made an appointment with my regular doctor for a pregnancy test. While in the office waiting for the results I was so nervous and was practically in tears, already assuming the worst. The nurse came in and reported a negative result which put me over the edge. I was a red-faced, crying mess by the time the doctor made it into the room. I explained how we had been trying for a while and that I was late in my cycle but the home test and now the office test all gave a negative result. Seeing how distraught I was, she went to double check the results and came back with news I wasn't sure I could believe. "Sometimes it takes a little longer for the accurate result. Although it is a lighter-than-usual coloring, it is still a positive," she told us. Recently, I was reading up on female hormone issues and learned that this test result could have been due to a low amount of human chorionic gonadotropin (HCG) hormone present. My hormones were definitely out of whack! This back and forth with the positive and negatives was taking my emotions on a roller coaster ride! While I was very excited that I was in fact pregnant, somehow it still didn't feel quite right. As much as my heart wanted to, my head wasn't buying it.

    I was only about two or three weeks along in the pregnancy but I decided to find a gynecologist that specialized in high-risk pregnancies. I am sure this was the prompting of the Holy Spirit. I am not so sure that my regular doctor would have recognized the red flags for what they were, the first being the low HCG level.[1] Less than a week after my first appointment with my new OB/GYN, I woke up with a ridiculous amount of pain in my lower pelvic region and could barely catch my breath. My husband was concerned and urged me to call the OB/GYN. I knew what I was feeling could not turn out well and that same uneasy feeling I had in the doctor's office returned. I knew in my heart that if I called the doctor I would not remain pregnant and the whole crazy roller coaster would start all over again.

By the time my doctor returned my call I had arrived at work. He told me to go straight to the hospital and that he would meet me there. Since I had gone to work that day hoping and praying the pain would pass, I had to then drive myself to the hospital. Mario met me there. As the doctor explained what he thought was happening, a feeling of nausea was churning up inside me with a dose of pain in my heart that I couldn't handle. He would have to run some tests to verify exactly what was happening.

My in-laws came to the hospital, my pastors came, a friend came, and Mario was by my side the whole time. None of them could do anything because God had already decided. This one was His. After what seemed like hours of being poked, prodded, inflated, and deflated the doctor told me that he could confirm that it was an ectopic pregnancy. An embryo had attached to one of my fallopian tubes. Desperation began to set into my mind and I reached out for any inkling of hope trying to hear in his words that I would get to keep my baby. There was none.

Even though I knew the answer, I asked anyway, "Can't you just push it through into the uterus?" Surgery was inevitable or risk losing a tube and thus lessening my chances of any future pregnancy. He removed the embryo with surgery going in through my belly button and another small incision in my pelvic area. The physical scars are still visible; the emotional scars are still painful. The worst part was waking up knowing that there wasn't a baby. I felt empty.

While I tried to remain optimistic despite the hormones raging each month and the letdown after every menstrual cycle began, it was definitely a challenge. My body would not do what it was meant to do and I had no control over it. Just like many other things in my life that I had struggled with, here was one more that made me feel like I didn't quite fit in. I always felt like I wasn't brown enough to be half Mexican, I wasn't from the right side of the tracks to sit with the popular crowd in high school, and now I couldn't produce kids like other women, the natural way.

After another year on this emotional roller coaster, attending what felt like hundreds of baby showers, and hundreds more people asking when were we going to have kids, we decided to explore more aggressive fertility treatments. We went for a consultation appointment at a fertility clinic to explore our options. In doing research we found that the average success rate of live births using in-vitro fertilization is about 40 percent per cycle. At $15,000 a cycle, they were odds we couldn't afford.

I knew there were other ways to have a family, but it was at this point it struck me that maybe it was not going to be easy or natural for us. I wrestled with God over this. I couldn't make my body get pregnant. Eventually, I came to the realization that I had to give complete control of my desires over to God in order to know His will for us in building our family. I finally did this one morning during my devotional prayer time. I was so tired of the emotional drain, of trying to second guess God. I had finally come to a point where I was willing to surrender my will over to Him without any begrudging feelings or deal making. I prayed, "I give this to you, Lord. If kids aren't in the plans, then I'm going to trust that is your will." He knew what was best and I would be okay with whatever He decided. Almost immediately I was rewarded with feelings of contentment. In that small amount of time my perspective had shifted. I had two dogs, a wonderful husband, a beautiful home, and annual exotic vacations. If kids were not in the plans then I would be okay. I now realize that I had to let go of my dream to birth children in order for my dream of motherhood to even begin.

4
Sign Me Up!

I can't recall a specific conversation with my husband but I remember him trying to console me at some point during the roller coaster with a flippant, "Well we can always adopt." That casual comment unexpectedly slipped back into my mind in the beginning of the summer of 2006. We had a trip to Belize planned for August but I had two months to kill beforehand. As a school teacher with summers off, I was restless, so I began to explore adoption.

I think I just typed *adoption* in the web browser on my computer and started to click on different things that came up. I didn't have a clue about the process I was considering, much less the degree of scrutiny that is involved. I had only heard rumors about the astronomical fees for private and international adoption and so I first looked at state agencies. I saw a few things about kids that were legally available for adoption in other states through social services. When I read up on adoption through our state and county Human Services, I learned that there was not a way to circumvent the foster care system.

Our county requires that a family become fully licensed for foster care. Then, a child who is removed from his or her home for various reasons is placed in care with a foster family for a minimum of six months. If that child is reunified with the biological parents, then the foster family waits for another placement and another six months. If that child becomes legally available for adoption, the legal process continues as the foster family, social workers, and court work together to complete all requirements with that end in mind. That process could go on for a while and there are never guarantees.

I was trusting that God had a plan for us but I still didn't know if it involved kids. I thought maybe this avenue of foster care—that I was not open to—was a roadblock. I couldn't, at that time, imagine in my heart caring for a child that maybe would be yanked away from us after we were completely attached. In fact, this is probably the number one reason why many people say they can't do foster care or adoption. In retrospect, I see it was more of a traffic cone that was guiding us in a different direction. While I couldn't imagine going through that process, God could, in His perfect timing.

August in Belize was beautiful! A romantic getaway was perfect right about then—well almost. We were crossing Chetumal Bay in a water taxi over to Ambergris Caye. Our destination was the cute little town of San Pedro, which faces the Caribbean Sea and the Barrier Reef, when suddenly I started my period—again! By this time I had warmed up to the idea of adoption but my hormones were all over the place going crazy. I imagine I was like the scary witch in Hansel and Gretel following (with my eyes) all these cute native island kids, attempting to entice them with conversation (in my head) to come home with me. *Don't you want a nice mommy to take care of you and love you and give you everything you want? I'll buy you a puppy!*

The vacation was magical! We swam with Manta rays and Nurse sharks, we explored the beautiful barrier reef covered in vibrant colored coral and every fish imaginable. We went looking for manatees in the mangroves and looked for seahorses in the shallow waters. We ventured to other cayes and dined on delicious local fare each day. We swam in a blue hole, climbed ancient ruins, went spelunking on a cave tube tour, we searched for howler monkeys in the baboon sanctuary, and we pretended to be in a forest as we perused the loosely enclosed exhibits of big cats in the Belize Zoo. It was the only way we would catch sight of a black jaguar, our tour book informed us. We came home with a camera full of memories and a timeshare to boot! My husband said, "Maybe we could adopt from Belize!"

I came home and got another puppy which would have to fulfill the motherhood desires that would occasionally flare up. Instead of another bulldog, we got a Chihuahua; one I could dress up, hold like a baby, and snuggle with in bed. We had decided we would try adoption. We didn't know how to start, where to look, or what it would cost. It turned out to be extremely costly both financially and emotionally, but worth every tear and cent. The overwhelming amount of information and paperwork to collect, combined with the long wait and the unknown factors, were frustrating to the point of melting me down many times throughout the process. Nanea, my Chihuahua, helped me get through that time as many a night I hid my crying eyes in her fur.

After investigating a bit further, we decided it couldn't hurt to at least find out about some of the specifics of international adoption since the other routes (foster-to-adopt or private adoption) seemed to contain too many roadblocks. I began calling agencies in our area that specialized in it. After a few calls I realized that we would have to pay a minimum of $30,000 in fees and expenses for a wait of over two years in order to adopt a baby from China or Guatemala. The positive was that in 99.9 percent of the cases, the adoptive parents did eventually get to bring their child home. These odds were much better than the fertility clinic, but at double the cost!

I called one more agency and, after hearing the same thing, I asked with a slight quiver in my voice, "How do people do it? How do people come up with these huge amounts of money to cover the costs of international adoption?" This lady, sensing in my cracked voice that I was probably about to break down in tears, quieted her voice a bit and said, "It's amazing how God just provides along the way." Suddenly, I was feeling reassured and knew it was something to which we needed to give serious consideration. I had never met or spoken to this woman prior to this call but her few words inspired hope within me. God had spoken through her to direct our path and next steps.

Feeling confident, I got to work finding an international agency that could coordinate an adoption through Belize. Since we now had a timeshare in Belize and really loved it there, it seemed the ideal choice for us. This proved to be more difficult than I had thought. I found a small agency out of Arizona, International Child Foundation, that worked with many different countries. This agency was willing to guide us through the adoption system in Belize including the country's specific requirements. Adoption agencies also provide guidance on the mountains of paperwork that need to be completed and filed. Forms have to be filled out and documents submitted for state seals; doctors reports, a home study, financial forms and documents, and letters of references have to be obtained; and everything had to be notarized. The list was endless.

A friend of ours, Craig Juntunen, recently produced an incredibly well done documentary titled *Stuck.* Craig's goal is to show the reality of a dysfunctional international adoption process and how children can become literally stuck in the system for years. There is a scene in the film that shows graphics of stacks of paperwork and the narrator rattles off a huge list of all that adoptive parents must provide. The idea, I believe, was to convey the bureaucratic obstacle course of paperwork required to adopt internationally. I am a firm believer in following the rules but this part of the movie resonated with me. This excessive documentation was no small feat and seemed almost insurmountable to me at times. As I watched the documentary, I recalled the range of emotions I had personally felt as I trudged through each requirement, from excitement to feeling overwhelmed, frustrated, angry, and even hysterical at times. I couldn't fathom why certain things just couldn't be done in a more efficient, cost-effective, and common-sense way.

It took me eight months to get all the necessary paperwork together. I had more free time than Mario as he was working patrol by then. By the end of May I had every single piece of paper, every stamp, every signature required, all tucked neatly inside a large manila envelope. This 2-inch thick packet was our dossier. I was feeling accomplished and proud. Then the phone rang. It was the adoption agency. "I know you have your heart set on Belize, but there has been very little movement in their adoption program. Because they hardly adopt out of country, I have to recommend that you consider other countries for your international adoption." *Really? Eight months and now you tell me this!* My disappointment at the time didn't allow me to see that this was actually God, again, setting up a traffic cone, directing us another way. "Would you consider Haiti? We work with a small program there that is comparable in cost to Belize," she assured us.

Other than a paper on Haiti I had done in college, I knew little about the country. After finding out what the difference in requirements were as far as the paperwork goes, we decided to switch countries. It took another month to make the changes and to get the additional seals, and so forth. By the beginning of June our dossier was completely ready. Prior to this I had completed all the paperwork for buying and selling our condo and purchasing our house. However, that paperwork combined did not prepare me for the amounts of paperwork I would have to deal with for our adoptions. Only God knew I could handle it.

Elizabeth Molina

5
Matched!

Although it had only been a few weeks, the anticipation and not knowing what was next in the adoption process was killing me! Finally, in late July we got a call from our agency and were told our dossier had been received and approved. We were eligible to be matched! That meant that we could learn about the available children on the orphanage website and see what child we might be interested in adopting. It may sound like it's an online shopping session, but this had God all over it. From the moment we looked at the eight available kids, my husband knew which child was to be ours. The children's photos were on the website of an organization called Chances for Children. This was the U.S. organization that partnered with the Foundation in Haiti that ran the orphanage. They also facilitated the adoptions and fundraised for a number of other humanitarian projects. The first time Mario and I sat down and looked together at the pictures, he pointed to a photo of my oldest son and said, "That's my son." I was not as quick to commit.

It took me almost a week to realize it was God directing our steps through my husband. My niece was visiting with us that week. Early that weekend I returned her to her home and then her mother and I took off on an overnight girls trip to Balboa Island. It was supposed to be a relaxing weekend for my sister as she had finished teaching another stressful school year. I had convinced her to let me tag along. The whole time I kept going back and forth about which child to choose. Sure, I thought, this kid my husband pointed out was really cute. They all were. My tired sister listened to me that whole weekend excited for a new nephew to join the family.

We only had their picture and a brief explanation of their personality. I felt like it was not a decision to make quickly or one to take lightly. I wanted to think it through carefully and to analyze every aspect of what I could only assume each child would bring to our family. The possibilities swirled through my mind; maybe we should adopt a younger child so he is more moldable; maybe we should adopt a sibling set so we would each have a child to hold. I really did want a sibling set, but my practical husband said, "Maybe we should start with just one kid until we know what we are doing." Ultimately, I knew in my heart it had to be God leading us to make the right choice–His choice.

Upon returning with my sister to her home, I was still second-guessing myself about which child to adopt. I desperately wanted to know God's will. My niece had been a witness to all the discussions my husband and I had earlier that week. I asked her what she thought. I don't remember her exact words but it came across as very matter of fact: "Mario wants to adopt Gualège (KAH-lezj), right?" Taking a short mental trip back through the week I recalled that my husband had consistently pointed to our son's picture each time we went back to the website. It was at that moment the realization occurred that God had spoken His will through my husband. My heart was bursting with excitement.

I wasn't sure what the road to adoption would look like but I knew it wouldn't be without God's guidance. I later found out that the younger male child and male sibling set I had been considering were already matched with other families but the website had not been updated. Another traffic cone had been set. I told my husband at the end of that weekend that I agreed with him and that we should adopt the cute, little three-and-a-half-year-old boy. I could tell by Mario's smile and a sense of peace in my heart that this child was definitely part of God's plan for us.

Our request to be matched with our son was forwarded to Haiti. It was approved by the end of

August and then the real waiting began, which is a major disadvantage to international adoption. However, one of the advantages is that it is 99% a sure thing. I knew that it would take a while but eventually I would bring my son home. Meanwhile, I would get to know everything I could about the in-country part of the adoption process, the culture, and the language.

    I went to a French club that met at Barnes & Noble on Saturday mornings toting a picture of my son. In the minimal amount of French I had picked up backpacking through France in college, I excitedly explained that this child was my son but that he was in Haiti. Evidently my French was really bad because they all thought I was sponsoring this kid. I ditched the French Club once I learned that Creole was what most Haitians speak and that my son would not understand me if I spoke to him in French. Both languages are official in Haiti but Creole is what the majority of Haitians speak. French is taught in school along with Creole. Like many people who take the obligatory two years of high school Spanish in the US, Haitians who have gone to school seem to forget what little French they may have learned, as it is mostly spoken among the Haitian elite.

    More paperwork still had to be completed on both ends. We had to await approval of the adoption by the Haitian Social Service Department (IBESR) before anything else could happen. We learned that we could travel to Haiti to meet our son and file his U.S. visa there. This would allow him to come home on an IR-3 visa once the adoption was completed. This meant he would naturalize or become a U.S. citizen the moment he stepped on U.S. soil. This seemed to be the most efficient way to process that part of the adoption so, naturally, we jumped at the chance. We were very excited to see firsthand the birth country and culture of our son.

My husband and I both had traveled extensively in our younger adult years. He had seen most of the Middle East and many parts of Asia while in the military and I had lived in Spain for a semester and had backpacked through Western Europe and Mexico. Traveling to a foreign country was not a big deal for either of us. That was until we had to get all the shots needed. We had to be up to date on all our routine vaccines as well as boosters. Hepatitis A and typhoid shots were also needed and malaria pills were recommended. Despite my strong dislike for needles, I was very anxious to meet our son and so I got everything needed without a complaint.

Elizabeth Molina

6
Meeting Gualège

We planned our first trip to Haiti to meet our son around the time of my birthday in early November. These trips were coordinated by Chances for Children so that small groups of adoptive families from all over the US could visit their child at the orphanage for about three days. It seemed like too short of a trip, but they were purposely planned this way so as not to overwhelm the kids, orphanage staff, and even us, the adoptive parents. In that timeframe we would meet our son, file his U.S. visa application, and experience a tiny bit of the culture.

    We took a red-eye flight to Ft. Lauderdale and arrived early in the morning to meet up with other adoptive families and the trip coordinator at the gate of our flight. We flew out later that morning as a group and arrived in Port-au-Prince, Haiti, before noon. We stepped out of the plane and into what felt like a sauna. Hot air hit our faces the moment we passed through the door and onto the top of the ladder that led us down to the runway outside the main airport terminal. We walked about 200 yards to the entrance and were greeted by a small trio of musicians dressed in crisp white shirts and small red neck scarves playing some lively Caribbean music. This reminded me of the obligatory ukulele player and hula dancer I'd seen many times greeting tourists arriving at the airport in Hawaii. Quite a contrast from the dull, sterile environment of the Los Angeles International Airport.

Entering the Port-au-Prince airport, I was amazed at all the stares we got while walking through the terminal and waiting in line to get through customs. At first, I thought maybe they had mistaken me for a famous celebrity but then I realized it was because I was in the minority. I felt odd and out of place, but I was determined to fit in. In all my international travels I had always tried to assimilate as best I could, whether it be attempting to speak the language, adhere to the local customs, or just trying to look less like the ugly American stereotype. I knew from my experiences with international travel that our obnoxious reputation precedes us. I made my first feeble attempts at Haitian Creole when I got up to the counter and had my passport stamped. I think I said something like, *"Bonjou, koman uo ye?"* ("Good morning, how are you?"). My attempt was rewarded with a friendly smile from the passport agent and I was waved through.

Next, we made our way through the crowd of arrivals inside the terminal as we waited for our luggage. Adoptive parents brought supplies for the orphanage on these short trips. Each person traveling was asked to donate or solicit donations of supplies to fill the maximum number of baggage allowed. We brought cloth diapers, baby formula, medicine, and non-perishable food items like tuna and peanut butter. Securing all the extra luggage and boxes from baggage claim was another small feat accomplished inside the airport. This was my first experience with Haitian time. It was even slower than Hawaiian time. Everything was at a snail's pace and very relaxed.

I had read the emails sent to prepare us for each step along the way but, at the risk of sounding clichéd, nothing could have prepared us for what we experienced outside the airport. We were advised to hold on as tightly as possible to our luggage once we were outside the terminal doors and not to allow anyone to "help" us get our luggage to our driver and cars. It was difficult to hold onto it and not just because it was a lot of stuff. Once the doors opened to the outside of the airport there was massive shouting coming from the throng of people lined up trying to "help" us, begging to help us, or just simply begging. How could we say, "No thanks!" to the guy that looked 10 years older than his actual age, hobbling along with a makeshift crutch, trying to carry our bags, practically knocking us away from them so he could earn a buck? We had learned that most Haitians lived on a little more than a dollar a day. I couldn't even imagine what that was like! Who were we to deny him his daily wage? We were the *blans* (white people). Our skin color signaled one thing to a desperate Haitian: tourist dollars.

After making it to our drivers' cars and getting everything loaded, we caravanned out of the airport parking and through Port-au-Prince for a long drive to the orphanage to meet our kids. I had seen poverty in other third-world countries, but what I witnessed as we bumped along was not just pockets of poverty here and there on the drive. It was everywhere. It was the way of life for the majority. Then we would see a few school children in their impeccable matching uniforms walking along, not really fitting in, but certainly belonging. This stark contrast between the haves and have-nots was beginning to define Haiti for me. The course my son's life could take was like a lottery—and the odds were not in his favor.

A drive that would have taken less than 30 minutes in most U.S. cities took almost two hours due to the lack of infrastructure. The main road east out of the capital was two lanes, paved, and almost absent of potholes. We traveled about 50 mph. That road eventually went through a small town called Croix-des-Bouquets that was bustling with activity, slowing us down a bit, but very interesting to observe. We continued east and eventually pulled off that main road onto a dirt road, somewhat paved with rock, that would lead us to the scant village of Lamardelle in the community of Ganthier. The caravan slowed to almost 5 mph so as not to get a flat or to pull aside and make room for the massive trucks rumbling back to the main highway. Occasionally you would see a car stopped with the driver out in the middle of the road trying to pound in a few of the rocks that were not allowing for as smooth a ride.

We finally came to a part of the road that had a few one-room houses and other signs of a town. We saw a cemetery, a Vodou church, and then we wound through a narrow road with some small-scale abandoned buildings that were probably microsized storefronts at one time. I later learned this petite village was called Ti Mache Le Tellier. This was where they would hold a weekly market on Wednesdays, something similar to a farmer's market in the US, complete with a donkey parking lot. The difference was that this was the *only* market in the village for some of the people to buy, sell, or trade their small amounts of produce or homemade wares. When we came to a Christian church and modest open-air school building, our guide notified us that we were almost there. I would, on later trips, grow very excited seeing these familiar markers signaling to my heart that it would soon have respite from the pain of missing my son.

About 35 kilometers (just over 22 miles) after

leaving the airport, we pulled up to a large rolling solid-metal gate with what appeared to be a guard tower. The first driver in the caravan honked and a guard in uniform, shotgun in hand, came through the gate. Then he opened it, allowing all the cars in our group inside the crèche compound. The whole place was surrounded by a 15-foot brick wall with barbed wire and broken glass bottles for extra measure along the top. I learned later that all the extra security is necessary to protect the place from being robbed and looted for food and supplies. Rampant poverty can lead people to take desperate measures. Once inside the compound, after passing a large grassy area about the length of a football field on the left, we came up on a large solid structure with heavy metal double doors. There was also a garden, a small guest house, and a playground area on the right. The whole place was beautiful and lush with tropical foliage, appearing to me more as a place of respite than an orphanage, as it did not fit in to what I had seen of Haiti so far.

Despite not having slept for almost 24 hours, anticipation was growing in the pit of my stomach. *Would he recognize me from my picture? Would he like me? Would he want me to be his mama?* When we arrived, the kids were in their communal rooms waiting for us. My husband and I were taken directly into the older boys' room to meet our son. The big boys were all sitting on a blanket on the floor just hanging out talking and entertaining themselves. I have never been one to cry tears of joy but that day, that moment I was introduced to my son, I cried tears of joy. What I felt is hard to describe. I imagine it must be what some new mothers might feel when laying in the hospital bed and the baby they have carried in their body and heart for nine months is placed on their chest right after being delivered. I had carried his picture around and had loved him in my heart for five months. I was flooded with emotion when I finally got to physically hold him. It was a moment of finally, really feeling like a mother. I felt like I could breathe again, as if I had been holding my breath forever!

We were introduced to a tall, sturdy, handsome boy with beautiful light brown eyes whom we immediately recognized from his picture. He was reserved but seemed curious. I took the hand of Gualège, my son, and led him past the rows of wooden bunk beds over to a wall. There, hanging near his bunk to remind him of us, were the photo pages I had sent with our dossier. Although he was just four-and-a-half-years old, he was at least a solid 50 pounds! I lifted him up a little ungracefully onto my hip and I pointed to the picture of myself and then pointed back to myself and said the Haitian Creole words I had rehearsed over and over a hundred times at least in my car with the CD, "*Mwe se mama ou,*" ("I am your mama").[1] He stayed by me for the remainder of the morning, every so often looking up at the *blan* lady, probably not really sure of what was going on, but excited to finally have his own special visitors as he had seen his buddies experience so many times before.

He seemed enamored by me and interested in Mario, but still somewhat reserved. Soon after we started taking out all the snacks and toys we brought he readily came out of his shell. He was still kind of quiet, but spoke when he needed to even though we couldn't completely understand him. Of all that we brought, he mostly enjoyed our plastic water bottles and our sunglasses. Food was not lost on him. The boxes of sugar cereal were a favorite snack, especially out on the playground where it gave him some sort of leverage. We didn't completely understand what was going on all the time between him and his mates, but we could tell between the few words we did know, the tone of voice, and the gestures that it was his mama doling out the treat so he could dictate how it went down. At one point we watched him barter with a mate: a piece of torn latex balloon Gualège wanted in exchange for more snacks. He wanted to try to blow it up and pop it much like we do with bubblegum. We toured the crèche inside and out, meeting the local staff and at the same time trying to acclimate to the humidity and overcome the jetlag.

When it was outdoor playtime for the kids, my husband and I took a brief break inside our room in the guest wing. We tried to take a short nap. My son, Gualège, was not about to lose a minute of time with his special visitors and came pounding on our door after what felt like barely 10 minutes of shuteye. This was our first day on the job of being parents and we were already exhausted. We had been told ahead of time how packed the three days would be with late nights and early mornings. I realized then why the trips were so short.

Madame Coindy was the wonderful lady that managed the day-to-day operations of the crèche. She directed all the nannies and groundskeepers, security guards and preschool teachers, nurses and cooks and therapists, cleaning staff and drivers; all were under her direction. With all her responsibilities, she still took time to personally prepare our evening meals, sharing with us traditional dishes and recipes of Haiti. I could have lived on the beans and rice prepared Haitian style. It was delicious! Avocado and onion salad was dressed with oil, vinegar, and spices; chicken, pork, and goat were prepared with delicious rich sauces and always fried plantains. This was all included in our trip costs but was a stark contrast to the kids' daily meals.

Each morning, after getting ready for the day, Gualège would come bounding into the guest wing during breakfast and eagerly sit with us to eat. He then ate again with the other kids less than an hour later. He ate every bit of the cereal with watery powdered milk served to the kids. Lunch for the kids that day consisted of some sort of grain (sorghum or maize) with black bean sauce. Mango was one of the plentiful fruits and was often served as an afternoon snack to the kids.

Dinner was almost always the same every night for them; they called it *labouye*. It was a thick porridge made with flour, cinnamon, sugar, water, and powdered milk. While it is a nice dessert or treat before bedtime, it hardly sufficed as a regular meal for a growing child in dire need of nutritious food. These meals were not bad, because the consistent meals gave many of them a fighting chance. For the long term though, they were just not enough of the right nutrients to foster proper development in growing kids. They were, however, better than what the poorest of the poor of Haitian children experience. I had read about some desperate parents feeding their children dirt cookies. These "cookies" made of dirt, oil, salt, and occasionally sugar lack any nutritional value at all. The sole purpose is to simply stave off hunger.

    Most of the children in the crèche had distended bellies. This could be a symptom of Kwashiorkor disease or an infestation of intestinal worms. Kwashiorkor disease is a form of malnutrition caused by protein deficiencies in the diet, typically affecting young children. A symptom of it is fluid retention which can cause the belly to swell while the rest of the body is mostly emaciated. It is currently treated in Haiti with a ready-to-use therapeutic food (RUTF) consisting of mostly peanut paste and essential vitamins and minerals, and is called *medika mamba* (peanut butter medicine). Sadly, there are many Haitian children whose parents are not able to get help before it is too late. On the other hand, intestinal parasitic worms can be contracted from infected water or absorbed through the skin. Since the lack of clean water is a problem and many kids run around shoeless, it is easily contracted. This parasite lives primarily on the intestinal wall and eats up to 40% of the nutritional intake, thus also inadvertently causing malnutrition. A single dose of albendazole can rid a person of this nutrition robber. Although it is fairly easy and inexpensive to treat in the US, everything is a hundred times harder in Haiti. I don't know for sure what the cause was for their distended bellies. After all that I saw and experienced and felt that first day though, I didn't know how I was ever going to leave my child there. However, I had no choice.

That night after dinner we unpacked our donations, stacked and inventoried what was brought, took showers and finally settled in for what we hoped would be a good solid seven hours of sleep. Not to be so. By 4:00 or 5:00 a.m. we were awakened by the repetitive sounds of the Vodou drums. Just outside the crèche, a funeral procession made its way down the rocky road to the Vodou church and cemetery. Shortly after that the chickens and roosters were up adding their wake-up calls to the chorus. Finally, around 7:00 a.m., the cries of hungry babies and toddlers drifted from their rooms in through the windows of the guest wing. We were getting our first taste of parenting–a lack of sleep.

Today we would be meeting Mami Gina (as the

kids fondly called her), the director of the *Fondation Enfant Jesus*. The foundation included the crèche, the village school, a community program, and a church. I remember watching her as she walked across the entryway. I wondered how she ran all the programs and why she chose to. She was of the elite class in Haiti, educated abroad, and could very easily have chosen to enjoy a comfortable life in the United States, Canada, or even there in Haiti. She didn't. She chose not only to return to her birth country but also to dedicate her life to helping her people. I introduced myself and then she said, "Thank you for wanting to adopt Gualège. We have had a hard time matching him." Feelings of confusion swirled in my head. *Why would it be so hard to match him?* On his brief bio it said "strong-willed." That hardly seemed like a reason to pass up a child. Then it clicked–He was waiting for me. God knew our son would be relinquished and had chosen us for him long before he was even conceived. This is the case with God and believers. He has a plan and sets it before us. He gives us free will to choose our path. He even knows, long before we do, what path we will choose. I thanked God that day for setting us on the path that led to adopting Gualège.

    Our day was filled playing with all the kids, going down to meet Mami Duncan at her house (the village matriarch and Gina's mother-in-law), and a trip down through the community of Lamardelle on an ox-driven cart. This is when the extent of poverty in Haiti became most visible to me. The way 90% of the people of Haiti live was summed up on that ox-drawn cart ride. We saw the mud huts with roofs thatched with palm frond situated along the road; we saw the people going about their daily routine of bathing themselves or their kids or washing clothes in the ditch or river every which way we looked; we saw donkeys carrying loads of plantains and ladies balancing on their heads everything from baskets of fruit or other produce they were taking to market to sell, to buckets of water on their return from the community well. Then there was the brightly colored *tap-tap,* the public transportation system that would occasionally honk at anyone in the way, as though it could go much faster than us on the rock-paved road. We finally came to the end of the road that stopped right at the river. We took some time to stretch our legs, take pictures by the river, and try to soak in the country that we would attempt to remember for our kids.

    As an outsider, I could see poverty existed there in sharp contrast to my own well developed country. Although I believe every person should have equal access to obtaining the material riches they desire, I am not entirely convinced that the absence of a complicated, advanced, fast-paced society (that which allows one to attain said riches) is necessarily a bad thing. I could see the beauty in the natural simplicity of their daily life. I have attempted to simplify my own life many times. I don't claim to know the answer to this contradictory dilemma. Ideologically, I believe it lies in the balance, somewhere between meeting basic needs and retaining the beauty of a simple life. The Haitian people are strong, resilient, and determined; a people full of hope and a vibrant spirit. The simple beauty in the images of their daily reality are and forever will be permanently imprinted in my mind, and yet their needs burden my heart to this day as I attempt to reconcile the conflicting feelings within me.

    The next day the director, Gina, was to escort us to our U.S. visa appointment in Port-au-Prince. Along with us came a set of brothers from the crèche that had their final visa appointment. Gualège also got to come with us because he had a scheduled doctor's appointment. The car was packed and hot but the excitement of the little ones was contagious. The youngest of the little boys in the car was constantly chatting as he observed all the cars and trucks as we drove down the main highway. As we were driving along the chaotic streets of the capital we got stuck behind a fairly large *tap-tap* with lots of colorful pictures and wording painted all over it, including a rather large familiar picture depicting a black Jesus. Fahroul asked in Creole to no one in particular, *"Ki kote Jezi pral?"* ("Where is Jesus going?"). The innocence of his words garnered a brief laugh but his simple statement carried a lot of weight. In a place where poverty abounds, it could be easy for many to feel abandoned.

We arrived at the main offices for the crèche in Port-au-Prince. The converted two-story home was located in a decent neighborhood on a city street. As our driver pulled up the driveway, I noticed a Haitian couple sitting on a bench just outside the office. As we all unloaded from the car, the Haitian man called out, "Gualège!" and my son walked over to them to talk. Not knowing who they were exactly, my husband and I smiled and continued on into the office, which also served as a transit house for children being taken in. We met most of the staff and also took a tour of the house. While upstairs walking through the baby room, where children are housed until they are admitted and treated for any medical issues, we watched a nanny feeding a little boy. My husband thought he bore a strong resemblance to Gualège and said as much. I wasn't so sure.

We all finished our business in the capital late that day and headed back to the crèche towards the early evening. My son fell asleep in my arms on the ride back. As the sun began to set, my heart began to fill with an overwhelming love for a little boy I had only just met but had dreamed of holding for so long.

Elizabeth Molina

7
The Best Gift

The rest of the trip was filled with spending as much time as possible with our son, Gualège, while dreading the minute we would have to leave him. That moment would come as sure as the sun would rise and the roosters would crow. We rose early to pack the few things that would return with us, but mostly to eat a final breakfast together and to spend one last time playing with him before saying goodbye. It was explained to the children whose adoptive parents were there visiting that we needed to go and finish paperwork but that we would be back for them. I have no clue what was going through Gualège's mind or if he in the least bit understood it all. You would think it would be easier on the ones leaving, heading back to a place where there is always electricity and clean running water, where you get to choose what your next meal is going to be, where you are surrounded by the people you love and who love you, where life is so much easier and family stability and education is almost always a given. It wasn't easier for me. I would not have hesitated a second to change places with my son that day.

We were told that we could anticipate a call answering our questions about the couple at the transit house who knew our son and about the child in the baby room that resembled him. That call came just a couple of weeks after we were home. The young boy we had seen in the baby room that day was in fact Gualège's younger brother, Wakine (WAH-keen), and the couple that was there that day were their biological parents. We had been in Haiti for a little less than three days, but we were all there in the transit house at the exact time their birth parents were there to relinquish their son, Wakine. Of course, God's timing was perfect. He knew that they would also make the difficult decision to give up Wakine for adoption and He had chosen us to be his parents as well. God answers our prayers in His timing—when it is best. Sometimes we may think He's saying "no," but maybe it's a "not now."

I had forgotten about that moment way back in June when I was praying about which child(ren) we should request to be matched with. I had wanted a younger child or a sibling set! I can look back now and see how I had to relinquish my desires to Him and, in so doing, my will became aligned with His will. We proceeded in faith moving forward with adopting Gualège and I didn't realize, even after we got that call, that God was giving me the desire of my heart: Wakine, a younger child, and a sibling set.

My husband and I didn't have a conversation right then and there about whether we would also adopt Gualège's brother. We took our time processing it individually, bringing it up now and then, trying to feel out what the other was leaning towards. It was a decision we felt we had to make carefully, as there were many things to consider. Gualège had been in the crèche for a while already, just waiting to be matched. We had been told that to add another child to the paperwork would set the process back at least three months. In the larger scheme of things, and considering it took almost two years to complete the adoption, another three months is not much more to wait. However, we didn't want him to be there one minute longer than he had to. Studies have been done on the cognitive and emotional effects of institutional care on young children and the findings of these studies are not favorable. Yes, his basic needs of food, clothing, shelter, and safety were being met daily at the crèche, but what about his developmental and emotional needs? What would the long-term consequences be for extending his time in an institution? Orphanages and children's homes were never meant to be long-term solutions. Being unfamiliar with the whole international adoption process, our concern was whether it really would be just a few months longer. On the other hand, we had said from the beginning of the process that we would not want to separate siblings. What would be the best immediate decision for our son? God was looking at the long term.

We decided that I would take a second trip to Haiti for a visit in February of 2008. I was excited, since this time I would be going with a group of mothers that were also adopting from the crèche. We all left our husbands at home that trip. I was really looking forward to being with a group of ladies who could commiserate with my heartache. I was also hoping to befriend some that were further along in the process and who could shed some light on what I had to look forward to. Looking back, I see God placed specific women on that trip to guide my heart and steps.

Prior to leaving, my husband and I agreed that I would talk to Gina, the director, and find out exactly how the process would be held up for Gualège if we added in Wakine to our adoption. Based on her answers, we could make a more informed decision. Unknown to me, my husband had already decided in his mind and heart that we were going to adopt both boys.

Upon arriving at the crèche, I quickly found a couple of moms in whom I could confide. This was another short trip with a three-day turn around. We spent the first day playing with the kids, watching them while they ate their meals together, and observing their care and routines. I mostly engaged with Gualège that first day, but I would occasionally see Wakine sneak out of his room and yell in my direction, "Mama, mama!"

That night I brought up to the other ladies on the trip the possibility of adding in Wakine to our adoption. It must have seemed like a no-brainer to them, but it wasn't to me at that time. I needed them to help me process it all. My mama heart was conflicted. "Is it the money?" asked one. Just before I left we had finished our tax appointment and to our surprise, we had a sizable return coming to us. In that moment I realized that God had removed that obstacle. "Do you feel like you don't have enough love in your heart for both boys?" asked another. *Well, kind of. Do I? I don't know!*

I passed an English-speaking staff member in the guest wing and had a brief conversation with her about the decision my husband and I were trying to make. To this day her words are what I think of every time I see my sons together. "Elizabeth, the best gift you can give your son is his brother to go through this new life together." I went to bed that night feeling as though God was leading my heart in a direction I forgot I had once prayed for.

The next morning I woke early with the roosters and to the now-familiar sound of crying, hungry babies, and checked my email. My husband had sent me a message. *Tell Gina I want both of my sons to come home soon.* There it was again. Only this time I didn't need my niece to show me that God was speaking to me through my husband.

My mind and my heart didn't accept the news at the same time. My new mama heart was still wrestling with lots of thoughts. Was there enough love in my heart for both of these boys? Was it fair to Gualège to bring another child home? Would he be able to share our attention and affections? But in my mind I knew what I had to do. I told Gina we would like to add Wakine in to our adoption.

When I first asked Gualège if he would like his little brother, Wakine, to also come home with us, he shook his head, "No." I was feeling like I had already betrayed my son. God must have known I needed some reassurance because later that day, when I sat in his preschool room, the teacher, Mr. Jean introduced me as Gualège's mama, and then my son spoke out, "And Wakine's mama, too!" After that I felt a peace come over me, the kind you experience when you receive confirmation that you are in God's will.

Wakine spent the rest of the day pouring on the charm. He enjoyed throwing the ball around, singing and dancing, and he ate A LOT. Gualège was mostly reserved, but a very strong-willed and active boy. Wakine was very outgoing and comical. If he wasn't trying to get a laugh out of us then he would pour on the drama and try to get us to fall for his "sad" face.

Gualège was very protective of his younger brother. He always made sure Wakine was having fun and was in on the action.

Recently my older son said to me, "I'm just thinking what life would be like without Wakine." "I can't even imagine it. My heart would have a huge hole in it," I quickly responded. He is a sensitive, caring, and affectionate boy; compassionate, entertaining, and charming to all; creative, and a passionate athlete. Gualège is reserved, resolute, protective, curious, and a strong leader. My boys are as attached to each other as they are different from one another. I don't think they would really want to be without the other. God knew they needed each other. He also knew the desire of my heart, even when I had forgotten it myself.

Elizabeth Molina

8
Summer Lovin'

"You want to do WHAT?" was my husband's initial reaction when I told him I'd like to go to Haiti for a month. "I would like to do a couple of things for Gina," I said. She was looking for someone to develop and run a summer camp for the village school and we had also talked about maybe doing a teacher training program and perhaps a Bible study. I wanted to DO something for this country that was giving me my children. To sit idle while awaiting the completion of the adoption process was just not an option for me.

I wanted to help this country in the area that I knew to be crucial to their survival and advancement-education. This is something that many Americans daily take for granted. Our kids often dislike doing school work, we don't think twice about pulling our kids out of classes for an off-season vacation, and we easily put off college until we "figure it out." In Haiti, education is a luxury.

Haitians are well aware that education is the means to a better future. Yet many are unable to secure this better future for themselves or for their children. Public education is not readily available in Haiti. The task of educating the masses has therefore been laid in the hands of the private sector. The majority of schools are primarily run by religious organizations, non-governmental organizations (NGO's), or for-profit institutions. In addition to tuition, there are also the costs of uniforms, supplies, and textbook materials. Fortunately the NGO and non-profit schools fundraise and secure sponsorships for students. This allows many children to attend and to also have a meal or two while there. Yet some statistics show that, despite this, over 200,000 kids don't have access to education in Haiti.[1]

A friend had also planned to go to Haiti for the month of July to help with the summer programs and to do some other work for Gina as part of an internship. If it hadn't been for her, it may have been a struggle that month being the only *blan* at the crèche with limited Creole. My husband knew that my motives were not entirely altruistic. While I was anxious to go help out with the programs, I was also looking for a way to spend more time with the boys. This was the perfect way to do it. I could see them every day, learn their language and culture, bond with them, and give back to their community. It was all that plus a lesson in third-world living for us two *blans*. We agreed I would go. He flew there with me and stayed for the first week.

The church we were attending at that time had decided to sponsor my trip. They donated $500 to help with airfare costs, another $400 was collected and put toward personal supplies and food items, and $200 worth of Haitian Creole Bibles were ordered and purchased to send with me. Many people from our church also donated school and art supplies that I would be taking with me. I am always awe-struck at how faithful God is. For all the times I have seen Him work in my life or provide for me, you would think that it would no longer be a surprise, but it always is so amazing and such a privilege for me to see how He accomplishes His will.

Prior to leaving for Haiti, I had been working with the U.S. partner organization for the crèche, Chances for Children, to solicit donations and then load and send them off in a 40-foot shipping container. A local school district donated 300 school desks and chairs for the new village school that was being built in Lamardelle. Five hundred bags of school supplies came in from Utah, as well as much needed medical equipment from Idaho—all from other adoptive families. By the end of June, I had the container packed and sent off.

I had packed the huge duffel bags that would carry all the summer supplies I would be needing, and was mostly packed myself. I knew that it would be hot and that I would be out in the dirt most days. I would also be washing my clothes by hand so I didn't need to take much in the way of clothing. I packed some beef jerky, oatmeal packets, and some other high protein snacks that could suffice as a meal when needed.

After 36 hours of travel, 400 lbs of luggage, and a little over 3,000 miles, we arrived with the parent group that went out there once a month. After their three days and my husband's week, just my friend and I remained. We just sat there alone in the guest wing that first night and wondered if we would actually make it unscathed through the month.

I bunked at the crèche where I also showered and had some meals. I had been preparing myself since April for my trip to Haiti, knowing that I would not be enjoying the nutritious and filling meals of trips past. Those were parent trips. We paid for our meals and lodging. The circumstances of this trip were very different. I would not be paying for meals or lodging. The staff would be focused on caring for the kids. There was not a 7-Eleven up the road that I could run to. In anticipation, I started cutting down on the size of my meals so that I would not completely shock my body with such a radically decreased caloric intake. Consequently, I dropped ten pounds before I even left.

After the adoptive parents left, the meals at the crèche went from three full courses to just coffee and toast with peanut butter in the morning and an occasional meal at night. We both had packed some high protein, non-perishable snacks from home to have on hand. We also enjoyed many light meals at Mami Duncan's house. In getting to know her better, we learned that she had spent her life and her family's fortune trying to help her people there in Lamardelle. She owned the land on which the crèche, church, and school were built. Her personal residence was off to the side of the school, complete with a circular veranda and a swimming pool. We enjoyed almost daily use of the pool attempting to cool off that hot summer. But this was certainly not a rich lady living in grandeur among the poor. The whole property was a small, slightly rundown compound that had a look of once being a place of joy for her family to gather in. Now, much of her personal space was given up for the needs of the community. People would often come to her to seek help or work.

We didn't go hungry that month at all. We had no problem skipping a few meals, especially in 96° Fahrenheit weather with 63% humidity. We just weren't very hungry. We mostly drank water during the day with a small snack we had brought. We had light lunches that consisted of salad with avocado and fresh fruit and sometimes no dinner or maybe just some corn on the cob. I knew my stomach had shrunk even more and I felt the pounds melting off.

I weighed myself once on the scale in the nurse's office at the crèche and was so excited when I saw I had dropped ten more pounds! The nurse looked at me very confused. I was a crazy *blan* trying to lose weight in a country that struggles to maintain a daily average intake of 1,850 calories per person.[2] Compared to 2,260 calories for the neighboring Dominican Republic and 3,770 calories for the US, Haiti is one of the countries with the lowest daily caloric intake per capita. I think she thought I was even crazier when I told her I hoped to lose another ten pounds before going home. The reality is that it took her reaction to shift my perspective and to show me how potentially insensitive and self-absorbed that statement might have sounded. I knew I would eventually be going home to the land of over-abundance. But for many Haitians, this is their daily struggle.

    The summer camp was to be an enrichment program. One hundred kids had been selected from the village school to participate. Four Haitian men who worked in some capacity for Gina had volunteered to help. The regular school teachers, who would be participating in the teacher training in the afternoons, would also help out in the mornings. Of the four classes, I think the cooking class was the biggest hit. Each day the kids got to help prepare some small item like chips and salsa, popcorn balls, and even oatmeal cookies. As each group came to my classroom, I chose two or three students to be my helpers. They got to wear the aprons and demonstrate the steps as I directed. I didn't have a translator so I had to model each step. In one class, I asked a student helper to spray the baking sheet with cooking spray but I only held up the cooking spray. She didn't quite understand and when I handed her the canister she accidentally sprayed my face! After showing her the baking sheet she finally understood and sprayed it!

The gardening class was not very successful but they did enjoy working the soil with their hands and mostly playing with the water. If anything, they were left with garden plots for the regular school teachers or the groundskeeper to utilize. What seemed a novelty to me was not a completely unique experience to them. What I considered a fun hobby, was in reality the means of survival, for many there. The Bible and arts and crafts classes were a lot of fun, too. They re-enacted well-known Bible stories and created art with the materials I had brought. The last week of classes they worked on piñatas that each class designed. We stuffed them with candy I had also brought and then broke them. I think it was a strange concept for them (make a piñata, stuff it, break it), but they weren't opposed to it.

When I reflect on the summer program, treating the kids and teachers to some new experiences was fulfilling. Watching the kids carefully decorate their own cupcake only to gobble it down a short while later was precious. When I was showing the teachers how to make play dough we bonded over a moment of laughter when my own batch didn't come out right. The best part of the trip was the end-of-the-summer-program party that I held for the teachers and workers. The lady who cooks for the school kids, Madame Jestem, was there and she quietly asked me through the translator if she could have one of the Creole Bibles I was leaving with them. When I gladly handed her one; she was so thrilled that she hugged it to herself and repeated, "*Mesi ahnpil*" (Thank you very much) over and over. As an added bonus, the preschool teacher from the crèche brought over some of the older kids to participate in the camp as well, and so Gualège got to do "school" with me that whole month.

Many more adventures were to be had that month, including a ride with a propane tank in the back of a pick-up truck driven by an 83-year-old Haitian woman, four-wheeling through a cemetery, and a walk to nowhere littered with used shoes. I tried to keep friends and family updated on a blog that month when we had power and the Internet. Here are some excerpts:

Saturday, July 12, 2008
Going to the market

Today Mami Duncan drove us to the market in the little town just before Port-au-Prince. This 83-year-old lady is fearless! Before driving off her property she went into the church to say a prayer...I am glad she did! It was quite the adventure! I got to ride in the back of her pickup truck with Anne and Brittany, the other two American girls here for the summer, as well as Anne's translator, Alex. First, we bumped along the rocky road out of Lamardelle in the back with an empty propane tank we had to fill. Mami Duncan honked all along the ride but I wasn't sure if it was to say hi to the people along the way or to warn them she was on the road! We went to a small market in the town of Croix de Bouquets and then we rode back to pick up the propane and then also to buy ice at another store. Finally, on our way home we stopped at various stands along the way and Mami would barter with the vendor for a good price for fruit. On the way back Mami forgot to slow down for a bump and Anne and her translator almost went flying out of the truck as they were sitting on the propane tank that was rolling around. It was quite the adventure!

Tuesday, July 22, 2008
Field Trip

This past Saturday I had a very interesting day. I woke up at 5:30 a.m. so I could go with Anne, Alex (her translator), an agronomist, and a guide to a waterfall that supposedly cascades at the back of a valley. Well the first thing we did was try to get the horses ready. Anne's horse had a saddle (or piece of carpet that worked as a saddle) and was ready to go. Alex's horse was the one that lives here at the crèche. It took him and five guys to get a rope on it in the form of a makeshift bridle (the saddle was a piece of green carpet that looks like artificial grass for a putting green) and my horse was waiting for its saddle but then someone took off on it. We went to find it and did but it was taking too long to find a saddle so I said I would just ride it like that. This would not have been much of a problem riding bareback in the US but in Haiti feeding your animal comes after feeding yourself, and so this horse had not been very lucky lately. His spine was a pain in my behind—literally! Finally we were all ready to go and began our caravan through the fields of Haiti and crossed a trace of a river. We came upon the marketplace and the sight was straight out of a movie! Massive amounts of Haitians all at market selling, buying, trading, washing clothes, washing themselves, and socializing. We continued our trek following the trickle of river and had a trail of Haitians following us. As the horses were quite uncomfortable for us after a while we took turns riding and walking. At one point the three Haitians accompanying us were on horses and the two *blans* were walking. People stopped them and asked, "How come the *blans* are not riding the horses?" This was very confusing to them. We zigzagged through the valley crossing the water often but alas we did not make it to the waterfall. We asked many along the way how far or how long a walk was it but got many different answers. Some said it was a two-day journey and others didn't know...yet they were all heading in the same direction as us! Finally the guide and I stopped, placed one of the make-shift saddles on the ground to sit on, while Alex went on to catch up with the others and to turn them around. We must have been quite the sight sitting there. The *blan* with the 80-year-old man sitting on rocks in the middle of the river, eating apples together. Not knowing much Creole, somehow I was able to make conversation with him. We shared not only an apple but also some sunscreen and then we sang a song in Creole that Alex had taught me on the way. The song translates, "One kilometer by foot, uses, uses, one kilometer by foot uses up my shoe. Two kilometers by foot, uses, uses...." and on, and on. The guide sang it with me and every time we came to the end of the song we would find a used up, dead shoe in our path.

Monday, July 28, 2008
Four Wheeling Through a Cemetery

Haiti is a place that does not lack in adventure...ever! On Sunday, Gina took us to the supermarket, which was more like a convenience store. It is about a 45-minute drive from here. So we were all getting ready to get in the car and then the car wouldn't start! At first we all pushed it to try to pop the clutch but after many unsuccessful attempts Mami Duncan gave us a jump start with her truck. At one point we had an 80-year-old man helping us push the car! So finally we were on our way down the bumpy road and came upon a huge truck in the middle of a road with its tire stuck in the rocks on the road. The driver could not move the truck and so a traffic jam developed. As we had to get to the store before it closed at noon, we became a bit desperate and impatient. Finally, some guy showed us a way to go around. Now this was not a side road. It was four-wheeling through a cemetery with at least an 80-degree incline! Gina put the car in four-wheel drive and we all jumped out to guide her through the rocks and dirt and weeds and tombs. Finally she made it around but only after running over numerous headstones and a Vodou doll in the dirt!

. . .

Every day after I finished the morning classes I would grab my swimsuit and jump into Mami Duncan's pool to cool off. Sometimes I would bring the boys. At first Gualège wasn't sure what to make of it, never having taken a bath in a bathtub. All the kids showered at the crèche, and most Haitians living in the countryside would either bathe with a bucket of water or in the shallow parts of a river or the ocean, depending on what was closest. Gualège didn't really know that he could control his body in the pool instead of just letting the water pull him this way and that. It didn't take him long to figure it out but the first few times were a little scary for me. Up to this point I had grown fond of Wakine but I still didn't feel like I had a deep connection with him as I had with Gualège. That changed one day when we were in the pool together.

    It was another blazing hot day. We were going to be dripping wet whether we were in the pool or out, so why not stay cool? I had decided to bring the boys to the pool with me that day. Gualège was five-and-one-half years old by then and Wakine was almost three years old. They were both fairly tall boys for their age and Gualège could easily walk around the shallow end by now. I took Wakine in my arms and we swam around for a little while. At one point, I held him up out of the water with my hands under his arms and the sun was shining brightly behind him. His head blocked out most of the sun but its rays were radiating from behind him creating an effect similar to the crown on the Statue of Liberty. It was at that exact moment, when I was looking up at that blubbering, water-spouting, pot-bellied toddler, that he stole my heart. I fell in love with him. And right then, I understood that he was the baby I had desired the summer before. God gave me my desire and my heart was full.

By the end of the month I had bonded with my sons, learned to communicate in broken Creole, and had dropped fifteen pounds. I also had a plan. I needed to learn to speak Creole fluently so that I could communicate with the Haitian people and help my sons retain their native language once they came home. No problem.

Elizabeth Molina

9
I'll be Back

Even before getting on the plane at the end of the month that summer, I was already thinking about when I would be back. Now, more than ever, it was killing me to leave my kids. I had bonded with them, fallen in love with them, and snuggled and hugged and kissed them a billion times that month. My mama heart ached for these affections that I longed to give them, but that they would not have while I was gone.

    I couldn't really explain to them why I had to leave them, but I promised them a million times, "I'll be back." How do you explain to a toddler and a five year old, in terms they'll understand, that there are people and documents that are holding them up from joining their forever family? They had seen other adoptive parents leave and return and they had seen their friends leave forever. When would it be their turn to go with their forever family? My heart imagined them wondering this, but maybe their little minds were just really confused by it all.

Coming home was exciting for me after being gone for a while. Most of the plane ride back was spent guiltily daydreaming about all the food I wanted to eat, the food I had missed, the food I would try to steer clear of. My husband picked me up at the airport and we stopped at a Denny's along the way. I settled on a plate of nachos. I couldn't finish even a third of it! Yet my kids were still eating almost the same thing every day with not enough fat or nutrition to provide for their proper development.

I felt that this conflicting fact had to be reconciled, yet there was nothing in my power I could tangibly do to change it at that time. I prayed for their health, safety, and development. My pastor and his wife continually led our church family in prayer for our boys. Recently, my oldest son asked me about the effects of malnutrition and wondered, "If I had left Haiti earlier would I have the learning issues I struggle with?" My heart breaks for him that I didn't know how to do more at that time to help prevent the developmental issues that now have manifested. Since then, I have studied and learned about the many ways to support the children of Haiti. My heart is with the organization that coordinated our adoptions, Chances for Children. I try to support their efforts as much as possible. I also try my best to make up for the loss in my son's diet now and have educated him on how important proper nourishment is for the body and mind.

I was returning to civilization as I knew it, feeling like life in the US had just stopped while I was gone. But it hadn't. My sister was getting married that first weekend and I had to prepare a presentation and slideshow of my trip to report back to my church. The school year would be starting in a couple of weeks. The slow-paced lifestyle of Haiti, which I enjoyed while there, was in stark contrast to the busyness of my life in the US. I was glad to be kept busy, however, so as not to shed too many tears from missing the boys while sitting idle.

One of the lasting effects of the trip was a heightened awareness of food. I noticed it everywhere I went. I noticed the amount of food being served, the amount being eaten, the amount being wasted. I couldn't help but feel guilty myself if I couldn't finish a meal. As it was, I grew up poor and was already hypersensitive about food. Most days as a young child we had very few options, if any in our kitchen. Often times when I was in elementary school I would walk home during lunch time just so that I wouldn't have to sit and watch the other kids eat their sack lunch. I knew there wasn't really anything in the refrigerator or cupboards to eat but at least I wouldn't have to get the pitiful stares and questions from the other kids. Now, having seen firsthand my own kids' lack of food made it all the more personal. It is hard to talk to Americans about our abundance and the poor stewardship of food because, unless you see it and experience it first hand, it's difficult to fully comprehend.

School started and the seasons passed quickly as they do in the classroom. By November, the aching of my heart was too much to bear, especially not knowing how much longer it was going to be. The questions were gnawing at my mind, *When will I see them again? When will they come home? Will they ever come home?* I started to doubt. After a while, a dog just doesn't cut it for some of us. I wanted my boys. My husband didn't completely get it but he held me the long nights I cried for my sons.

I turned 36 in November of 2008. My biological clock had become a faint ticking sound that I hardly recognized, but my mama's heart was heavy. I was determined to visit the boys again soon and planned to return in December for their Christmas celebration. The parent group going that month would organize this for the children and staff of the crèche. I was able to occasionally talk with my oldest son by calling the preschool teacher on his cell phone, but it was not an easy task and so it was just a few moments here and there to temporarily comfort my aching heart. The next time I got a chance to talk to him on the phone I could only squeak out the words, "I'll be there for Christmas!"

Loaded down again with donations and gifts and

food supplies and diapers, I made the trek back to Haiti like an old pro. This time I was prepared. I had picked up quite a bit of Creole in the summer. I had continued to work with the Creole CD on my drives to and from work. Speaking their language helped me to feel connected to them in some way, even if I was only repeating phrases back to a lady on my car stereo. I witnessed other adoptive parents, who were just a few months ahead of us in the process, come to take their children home forever. I felt like it was getting closer for us. After almost a year and a half of waiting after being matched, and ten months prior to that getting all the paperwork together, I ached for that day to come.

Like all the other trips, it was surreal but short and crammed full of activity. I spent as much time as I could with the boys learning to be their mommy. I bathed them and dressed them, played with them and read to them and of course took lots of pictures. They animatedly acted out races and accidents with some toy cars and motorcycles I had brought for them. I talked with them and helped them in their preschool room. By this fourth trip, I was pretty comfortable with them but they still found this *blan* quite the novelty and enjoyed playing with my hair and anything I had with me.

The Christmas party was a lot of fun! The kids each got to open a present, although they would all end up in a community playroom. They heaped their plates with food from a buffet table the adoptive parents had prepared. Their eyes were huge as they enjoyed all kinds of treats and food they normally didn't experience. Abundance–yes. Waste–definitely not.

I returned home once again with a heavy heart unsure how much longer it would be. We knew there were about four or five different stages through which our case had to pass. Each of those stages could last a while. By now we had spent more than half a year preparing our dossier and another 18 months just waiting. Our files had been approved and had exited IBESR, the Department of Social Services for Haiti, and had been signed off by the judge at the children's court (PARQUET); we had applied for Gualège's U.S. visa when we went on the first trip and then I had applied for Wakine's visa over the summer; the Ministry of the Interior (MOI) needed to sign off on it and then passports had to be applied for. I knew we were getting close but I wasn't sure what that looked like in real time. And so the waiting game continued.

10
Bittersweet

"Friday is going to be my last day," I blurted out, trying to contain my excitement. I got off the phone with the agency and I wanted to climb up on a table and sing Hallelujah! It was a Tuesday afternoon and I was sitting in my classroom talking with my principal and another colleague when I got the call. "Get your plane tickets! Their U.S. visas will be ready by Friday," I was told. And just like that, after a 30-month process, we were going to be parents.

    I couldn't believe it! I was excited, nervous, and panicked all at once. The day I had been waiting for was finally here. Their room was ready, their closet and drawers were full, their book shelves were stocked, and their toy boxes were filled. The waiting felt like an eternity, but getting everything ready for them helped it pass just a tiny bit quicker. We had painted their walls a calming, muted blue and got them each a sport-themed bed set. We hung bamboo shades and stained a book shelf and armoire to match hand-me-down bunk beds. A rustic painted sign that said, "THANK HEAVEN FOR LITTLE BOYS" completed the room.

    There was so much to think about. There wasn't a list of items to buy or register for like the traditional expecting parents. I bought a handful of outfits for each of the boys. I knew that wasn't going to be enough unless I planned to do laundry every few days or so. Thankfully, my sweet friend mailed me a collection of her boys' gently used clothing, all the way from Hawaii. That was a huge help and relief. We had some toys we had been given at a group baby shower my coworkers were thoughtful enough to include me in. And since I didn't plan on returning to the classroom right away, I brought home my personal collection of children's books. Other than plane tickets, we thought we were prepared.

    My husband had a work event in Nevada that weekend. I got everything ready including booking flights, making hotel reservations, and packing the bags. The boys would not be coming home with a single personal possession from Haiti. Everything at the crèche was community property. How does a child so young handle that? When I packed up my bags to get ready for a semester abroad while in college, I passed out! I had a few anxiety attacks just thinking about leaving behind everything I knew to go live in a completely foreign place! How would their little minds handle it?

Mario returned from Nevada on Sunday afternoon and we flew out the next morning to Florida. We spent one night in Ft. Lauderdale and on Tuesday morning we flew into Port-au-Prince. On the way over, a flight attendant asked us the nature of our travel to Haiti. We told him we were taking our final trip to bring home our adopted sons. Our excitement was contagious and when we approached Port-au-Prince getting ready to land, we heard him announce our plans over the speaker system and were congratulated with applause from a plane full of people.

Bumping down that familiar rock paved road, passing the eerie Vodou church, pulling up to the beloved crèche...it would be the last time I would see these familiar landmarks that had caused the excitement of seeing, holding, and kissing my boys to stir up in me on each trip. Now, a small, uncomfortable –yet inexplicable—feeling was starting to form down in the pit of my stomach.

It was a school day and Gualège was at the village school in his Kindergarten class the morning we arrived. Wakine was at the onsite preschool with Mister Jean, their beloved teacher. Once Gualège arrived back at the crèche after school, we hung out as usual and made our rounds of the kids' rooms. The boys told all the nannies that they would be leaving the next day.

Some hugged them and shed a few tears, while most smiled. The boys handed out small gifts for everyone.

Madame Lefoe, the new onsite manager of the crèche, asked the boys what they would like to take with them on the airplane as a snack. She said she prepared a special treat for all the kids to take with them when it was their time to go home. I was imagining some muffins or some sort of special pastry. My sons asked for *kann* (KAHn) and *kasav* (kah-sahv): a piece of sugarcane and something that resembled a tortilla made from flour from the cassava root. The boys were thrilled. I wasn't sure how we would get the sugarcane past the customs inspection. It turned out we just needed to declare it on a form and put it through inspection before carrying it on the plane with us. The boys did not let that piece of sugarcane out of their sight the whole way home.

The plan was to spend the night at the crèche and to meet up with the boys' birth parents in the transit office in town the next morning so they could say goodbye, then we would be off to the airport. This last visit with the birth parents was optional but in my eyes, necessary. I couldn't leave without reassuring them that we would love and care for their boys as if they had been born to us.

The next morning was a busy one for everyone. I went up to the village school to visit with the teachers whom I had trained over the summer. One of them was very proud to show how she had begun to incorporate some of the methods she had learned from my training. We took pictures and exchanged emails, hugs, and kisses, and promised to stay in touch. The uneasy feeling in my stomach was getting hard to ignore.

    The nannies were all sad to see the boys go but at the same time happy for them as they were about to begin a new chapter of their life. Then the cooks, cleaning ladies, groundskeeper (Papi Joe), and even the guard all said their goodbyes. Finally the nurses, Mister Jean, and Madame Lefoe said their final goodbyes to the boys. At this point I imagined the boys had to have had some idea of what was going on but they weren't showing much emotion. The staff had begun preparing them a couple weeks prior to the transition. This simply meant that they told them what was going to happen in terms they could understand and answered any questions they might have. The boys kept asking me and then telling everyone they encountered that they were going to ride on a big airplane. I knew the weird feeling in my stomach was signaling something but I couldn't quite figure it out yet.

    By the time we were in the car and driving away from the crèche compound for our last time, the sick feeling at the bottom of my stomach was overwhelming. The feeling grew stronger as we approached the transit house in the capital city. My emotions were all over the place: the excitement of finally beginning the parenting phase of our lives, some self-doubt (because what if we couldn't handle them?), an almost natural defense mechanism sprouting up in the form of caution (we still had to meet up with the birth parents and what if they changed their minds?), and a tiny bit of nervousness (because you never know what will happen in customs at the airport in Haiti). Sure, this was going to be a huge change in our daily lives. We were aware there would be many adjustments along the way and we would have to be flexible. We knew we loved our boys and wanted them with us. Yet there was something more causing me to feel sick to my stomach.

I had come to love this country and its people. From it came the most precious little ones in my life, my boys. To suddenly not see the familiar faces of the Haitian people, to know that I may not return for quite a while, being fully aware that my boys would be leaving all that they had ever known in their short lives, to know that they would probably want to assimilate with their new culture which could mean losing their language, to know that their memories would fade and they may not want to identify as Haitian...it was all too much. At that point I finally understood that sick feeling in my stomach: I was grieving for my loss and for my sons' losses. I promised myself that I would do everything I could to help them retain as much of their language, culture, and memories as possible. This was as much for me as it was for them.

When we arrived at the transit house, the four of us were escorted to Gina's office and awaited the birth parents. Gina was not available to be our translator that day. The lady filling in was about as fluent in English as I was in Creole. We were also disappointed to find that the birth mother had not accompanied the birth father to say good bye. From what we could gather, she had stayed behind because she had just given birth to another sibling a month prior but also had other children at home to care for.

Many people have asked me why she would continue to have kids if she already gave two of them up for adoption. A plausible explanation, based on what I have read and learned from extensive trips to Haiti, is that women have an inherent value based on their ability to reproduce children. This is true in many third-world countries. If women are unable to reproduce, they may be cast aside. In rural areas, these children will help to provide and care for the family. In a place with such a high mortality rate due to the lack of medical care, coupled with extreme poverty that 98% of the country faces, chances are that not all the kids are going to make it past their fifth birthday. Add to that an illiteracy rate of almost 50%, a lack of education in birth control or a lack of available forms of birth control, and the influence of the Catholic Church on the use of birth control, and you have a crisis of great proportion.

Other people have asked me what happened to their birth parents. In other words, why did they willingly give up their children? This brings to the table the issue of adopting children who have living parents versus true orphans. I often compare it to a young mother-to-be here in the US who chooses to give up her child for adoption. She seeks out a family through a private agency or attorney. Her hope is to provide that child with all the opportunities for a happy, fulfilled life by placing him or her in the care of loving, stable parents. Not a decision taken lightly, she too feels that she is unable to provide this quality of life for her child and that this is the best option. We as a society have come to see this as acceptable and more preferable than some of the other options.

There are numerous individuals and organizations who have equally numerous opinions on the topic of international adoption and specifically the adoption of those children who have living parents. These arguments range from preserving the biological family unit, to preventing the loss suffered when removed from the birth culture, to child-trafficking. All of these arguments are valid. Also important to recognize is that these children are the future leaders, doctors, and scientists of their country, and that adoption potentially diminishes that talent pool. Finally, no country wants to admit that they can't care or provide for their own people.

Mario and I tried to put ourselves in the birth parents' position: If I knew that I could not provide even a glimpse of hope for a future for my children whom I love so very much, then I would probably do everything I knew to do to provide them that opportunity. This is a very hard concept for most Americans to comprehend because we have a welfare system and a whole slew of other social services that make it hard to argue the case. Often our situations are not as dire. But that is not the case in Haiti. Many times it IS a matter of life and death. There are no governmental social safety nets in place in Haiti that provide birth families with options to remain together. Thankfully, there are many organizations that are starting to look at alternatives to parents relinquishing children and are actively working to help birth families remain together.

Humanitarian and religious organizations have set up children's homes and orphanages. These were originally meant as temporary solutions and, when used appropriately, remain a vital part of the solution. However, many are used long term, creating problems with far more devastating mental and emotional consequences. I don't believe relinquishing children is the only way to resolve the issue of poverty, nor do I believe that it was God's plan for their biological mom to birth them specifically for me. However, I can't deny that God, in His perfection, orchestrated the adoption of our boys and thus the building of our family. He took a situation and made good come of it, as He is in the habit of doing. That didn't make this last trip any easier on my heart though.

The birth father was very kind, polite, and

gracious. He appeared to love his children, even traveling all night on a boat to get there to say goodbye. We asked questions about him and his family and learned that our sons had other brothers and sisters. The birth father talked mostly to the boys. From what we could gather via our translator, he shared what his hopes were for them in this new life. He and the birth mother hoped they would do well, be educated, and have a good job. It was very clear how much their father loved them.

  When it was close to the time for us to leave for the airport, the translator advised the father that he should say his final goodbye. He hugged the boys and kissed them on their little cheeks. We took pictures together and he proceeded out the office door. Wakine trotted after him but then stopped right before the doorway watching his birth father leave and then looked back at us. It was almost as though he understood what a toddler could not possibly be expected to comprehend. Standing halfway between us and the doorway, the only father he ever knew left him. The single tear that rolled down his chubby cheek dealt a blow to my new mama's heart that left me breathless. While in my mind I knew God had a plan that involved bringing a family together, at that moment my heart read it like a family broken apart.

11
The Firsts

We rushed off to the airport shortly after saying our final goodbyes to their birth father only to find ourselves waiting for hours in the airport. You would think this would be a difficult thing for three- and six-year-old boys to do, but it wasn't for these little guys. They took it all in, trying to entertain themselves quietly with water bottles, our sunglasses, and the few toys I had brought with us for the trip home.

    I can only imagine what was going through their minds as they sat there. Where were the *blans* going to take them? Would they return to the crèche? Why didn't their birth father come with them? When would they get on the big airplane? I could not tell what they were thinking. After five trips to Haiti over the course of two years, one being a month long, and listening to the CD over and over in my car, I had learned enough Haitian Creole to communicate with them. But no matter how well I could speak with them, there was no way to help them fully understand.

As I look back on that momentous time in our lives, I wish that I had been able to make them understand what my intentions were: to love them and to give them all the opportunities that were almost nonexistent in their birth country; what I believe their birth parents intentions were: to give them a hope for a future and all the opportunities that they themselves could not give them; and what God's intentions were and are for their precious lives: to know Him, to love Him, and to spread His love even to their birth family and country one day.

I have read that many birth parents in Haiti have a different understanding of what adoption really is. The birth parents might see adoption as a temporary guardianship instead of the permanent placement that the courts state. Their belief is that one day their children will return to Haiti with education and the ability to help them and to better their birth country. I'm not sure that their belief is entirely inaccurate. After all, aren't all our children, biological or adopted, on loan from God anyway? Returning to help Haiti has always been part of our plan with the boys and they are well aware of this. We said as much to the boys' birth father at the final visit. To this day it is still our hope for our boys to one day be reunited with their birth parents and biological siblings. As a family we hope to help in such a way that the lives of Haitians are improved, so that the cycle of poverty is not repeated with each generation, and so that Haitian mothers and fathers can keep their children instead of feeling as if adoption is the only answer.

As we waited for our plane to arrive, we sat and talked and walked around and shopped in the little airport shops and ate, and finally, after what felt like a day, we began boarding the plane. The boys were so excited! We got settled into our seats and the excitement grew. I could tell because they started to talk more to each other and to ask us questions about the many new things they were seeing, partly speaking and partly pointing, whichever took the least amount of time to get an answer out of us.

Just as the plane was almost completely full and almost ready to take off, there was a not-so-friendly discussion between some passengers and then eventually a flight attendant stepped in to attempt to resolve the issue. To the boys' dismay, we sat on the plane for another two hours waiting for the disgruntled passenger to disembark. By then we were exhausted! Although the boys were well behaved, the energy they had was way more than we had ever dealt with for extended periods of time. The fact that there wasn't a break in sight for at least another 15 years began to sink in. And this was just the beginning!

The plane eventually did take off that afternoon

and landed two hours later in Miami. Another few hours through customs and then a shuttle to our hotel had us arriving at about 10 p.m. Florida time. We could tell the boys were hungry. We were all sticky and exhausted. It was time for a quick warm bath, some dinner, and into bed. For the first time our little instant family was alone together. Those first moments are permanently imprinted on my mind and heart.

There is nothing like watching a child experience all their firsts. Traditionally, new moms record all the firsts in a baby book. The first bath, first word, first haircut, first step are all precious milestones in the parents' minds. The firsts for our boys were slightly different but just as exciting for us new parents to witness.

I didn't think twice about running them a warm bubble bath and certainly didn't anticipate the shrieks I would receive when I put them in it. They were so loud we were afraid we would get in trouble with the hotel. They weren't fearful yells or even yells of jubilee (although that's how I feel when I sink into a warm sudsy bath). Maybe they were pleasantly surprised. They were experiencing something for the first time and didn't really have a point of reference for it. Due to the heat and humidity in Haiti and the lack of running water for many, a warm bath was an entirely foreign experience for them. They eventually got over the excitement and sank into the tub and enjoyed playing with the water and bubbles for a while.

My husband had called room service and had ordered them each a plate of spaghetti. They had tried spaghetti before at the crèche but it was made with ketchup instead of actual marinara meat sauce. The red mountain of food that sat in front of them was four times the amount of food they had ever had at any one meal. A child their age from a developed country would have taken a few bites and walked away. They ate every bite of it. It was an incredible feat to watch! We later found out that they had parasites that may have caused them to feel so hungry, in addition to the malnutrition they had experienced up to this point.

At the crèche they had shared a twin size bunk with a mate. The hotel bed they were going to share was more like a bounce house. After about two minutes of jumping and playing and laughing on the bed they crashed from exhaustion. They sank into the white fluffiness that was their bed that night and quickly fell fast asleep. We, too, were exhausted but content to finally have our boys!

The next morning was an early one as we had to catch our flight to Dallas, Ft. Worth, and then a connecting flight to Los Angeles International. After that, we would be home. Another day of travel on shuttles, sitting around airports, and sitting in planes was too much excitement for our little guys. They fought to stay awake the whole day so as not to miss a single thing. Finally, as we were approaching our descent to LAX, they fell asleep on the plane. It was still somewhat early when we arrived in Los Angeles so a short nap was good for them.

Once we were all piled into our truck we headed down the Pacific Coast Highway to our little corner of Ventura. The Santa Monica Mountains sit on the right side of Highway 1 and the Pacific Ocean on the left. To a little three-year-old sitting in a booster seat high up in a truck it must have felt like he was about to fall into an abyss whenever we took a curve. A short while into our drive along the water Wakine began making a noise we couldn't quite decipher. It wasn't crying but it wasn't happy excitement. It sounded like a nervous exclamation in the form of excited, repetitive noises that sounded like "Why! Why! Why!" Between Wakine's agitations and Gualège calmly explaining to me in Creole, I was finally able to gather that Wakine was afraid the truck was going to fall into the ocean! We pulled over and moved his booster seat to the other side of the truck cab. This seemed to relieve his fears somewhat. We made it home without any other incidents.

Arriving home, the boys were curious and wanted to touch and play with all they encountered in the house. The TV buttons, light switches, door locks, drawers, cupboards, refrigerator— anything that looked like it was automated or contained something new to them was a source of interest and major entertainment. They were afraid of our beloved bulldogs, T-Bone and Patches, but seemed to like my Chihuahua, Nanea.

They loved having all the toys to themselves and played well together, keeping each other entertained.

They were very active boys. The first three days we were home I didn't get a chance to take a shower. The days were busy and I was getting used to a schedule of meals, play time, and baths, and the time just slipped right through my fingers. Having to teach a child every single thing and to explain it all in limited Creole was time consuming. Mario was still adjusting to fatherhood, too, and didn't really know that they needed constant supervision, and I was afraid to leave them alone.

One of the things they tell you in adoption preparation classes and adoption books is that, although chronologically they may be three and six years old, they are like babies in many ways and have to be taught everything as though they are learning it for the first time. This was the case even more so because they were suddenly plopped into an environment with a gazillion new things they had never seen or experienced. To say that it was overstimulating for them and exhausting for us would be an understatement. Most people get to ease into parenthood teaching their children new things little by little, with the child gaining a little more independence as each year goes by. Our boys had quite a bit to catch up on and they did not want to miss out on a single thing.

I think the light switches were one of the more fascinating things to them. In Haiti, the generator at the crèche wouldn't be turned on until the late afternoon. The light switches were probably not a huge source of entertainment for them there. Every time they flipped the light switch on in our house, the light would turn on! A few of our slider switches broke that first month after so much sliding on and off by the boys. I think they thought, "The next time I slide it or flip the light switch, it's not going to turn on." We are pretty good about paying our electric bill so the lights did in fact turn on—every single time.

Their first experience with certain foods was another amazing thing to witness and especially intriguing to me. I had grown up poor and, at times, homeless. The lack of consistent meals and always feeling hungry caused a lot of unhealthy eating behaviors to develop. Unfortunately, bad habits tend to die hard. Even after I grew up and had food security I was still prone to those early patterns. I didn't want my boys to have the same issues with food that I had developed, so I was very diligent in helping them to develop good eating habits and a sense of security with food.

Gualège would eat anything set in front of him as fast as he could and then hold his bowl or plate out to me and say, "*Ankò,*" in Creole meaning *again* or *more*. I would fill it up again and, after about three servings, he would finally be satisfied. Wakine would also eat very fast but, instead of uttering "*Ankò,*" he would pretend there was still food on his plate and continue to shovel his empty fork into his mouth. I would then offer him another serving which he would enthusiastically accept and gobble down. He was still kind of in the potty-training stage so we limited his liquids towards the evening. When he wanted more water and we said no, he would form his hand like an imaginary soda gun, like the kind bartenders use, and pretend to pour more in his glass and then proceed to "drink" it.

Often we would have to physically stop the boys while eating or pull food away from them. They were not sure how to eat certain foods like oranges and chicken drumsticks; they would eat every bit of the orange flesh and continue on with the peel. The same with the chicken drumstick—they would eat all the meat, the skin, then the tendons and even the cartilage, and then continue to bite into the bone itself and suck the marrow out. After a few of those incidents we learned to be more vigilant when we gave them something they hadn't tried before and that had the potential to confuse them. Later, when they were trying something new, they would ask me if they should eat the skin or certain parts of it.

For the first month it was recommended that we not go out too much so as not to overstimulate them. So for the first week, other than church on Sunday, we just went out to the park every day. It was the perfect place for two busy little boys and so much fun for them! They would ask every morning if we were going to walk to the park that day. Little by little we started going on outings to the grocery store and other places. Seatbelts are more of a vague suggestion rather than a requirement in Haiti. The boys seemed confused when we didn't move the car until theirs were connected. They were more like toys to them and often were disconnected in the middle of a car ride and so I would then have to pull over and reconnect them.

We decided to take them to a restaurant one day and thought maybe McDonald's would be a good low key place to start. We ordered Happy Meals for them. They were still eating like ravishing lions at that time but they seemed content with the meal and very excited about the cheap plastic toy that came with it, just as is every American toddler. They played with their toy for a few minutes after we were done eating and then we decided to head home. They asked me if they could take the toy with them or did it need to stay at the restaurant. The smile on their face went from ear to ear when they realized they could take it home, unlike the community toys at the crèche. McDonald's won that day but I had the final laugh. My boys realized that the food there wasn't as plentiful or as filling as it was at home and they came to prefer eating at home over the cheap Happy Meal toy.

I attempted to do some schooling with Gualège at home while Wakine played or napped. The first look I got when I asked him to look at a book with me was the most disdainful face I'd ever seen. You would have thought I asked him to pick up dog poop with his bare hands! The teacher in me was determined to help my child discover the joys of reading. They weren't discovered right away but eventually he did learn to love reading books and is now an avid reader.

After about a month of routines every day, we decided to change it up some and put Gualège in preschool for the rest of the school year (about six weeks). Although he had completed a half year of Kindergarten at the village school, and had two years of preschool at the crèche in Haiti, our plan was to have him repeat Kindergarten that fall at a private school. Not everyone understood our decision to hold him back, but it is not one we regret at all. He was engaged and learning many new things, he was immersed in an all-English environment (I was still speaking Creole with them at home), and Wakine got a regular nap as did I. My husband would be going back to work and I was gripped with fear as I didn't think I could handle it all alone. In fact, the first day Mario was getting ready to go back to work, I begged him not to leave me alone with them. He did, and we eventually figured it all out. Although Gualège was still probably overwhelmed by everything in the new culture, his starting school was good for all of us.

We had decided early on that on their legal documents we would give the boys a new first name, bump their birth name to be their middle name, and of course they would take our last name. We wanted them to have the option to revert back to their birth name later on. As a school teacher I knew how hard it was on some kids when their name was not pronounced correctly. I knew this would be the case for Gualège and possibly for Wakine, so we started using their new names, transitioning slowly.

My husband and I are avid basketball fans and chose names of two players we liked: Michael **Jordan** and **Grant** Hill. The boys seemed to like the idea of having the same name as talented basketball players. Now we use both first and middle names when we need to get their attention. I do hope they go back to using their birth names someday as they are such a significant part of their identity.

By the time Jordan (Gualège) started Kindergarten in the fall, he didn't want me to use his birth name or speak to him in Creole. From my graduate studies of second-language learners and students who migrate to the US, I knew this to be a step in assimilating with the new culture. I tried to keep them in practice with their native language. Eventually, it got to a point where they just looked at me with a confused look whenever I spoke to them in Creole.

That first year we enjoyed watching the boys experience life and seeing it all through their eyes. Their first visit to the doctor and the dentist, their first fishing trip, their first time painting Easter eggs, riding a horse, bowling, hitting a piñata, performing at school, watching fireworks, going to a birthday party, swimming at the water park –the glee in their eyes as they experienced even some of the simpler things was heartwarming. This delight seemed to me to be missing in children who come from more privileged situations. I've tried hard to preserve this in the boys but losing it is inevitable in the consumer-driven society in which we live.

We enjoyed a family vacation in Florida that fall that included a crèche reunion of sorts. They got reacquainted with many of their friends that had been adopted into families in the US. They were reunited with the crèche manager Mami Coindy and Foundation director Mami Gina, both whom they loved very much. I think the reunion was as important for me as it was for them. It seemed to help ease some of the grief I felt after leaving Haiti for the last time; I'm sure it was comforting for them to be with their friends who were experiencing all the same firsts.

Grant (Wakine) turned four years old that first October. For his birthday I decided to only invite the boys next door and our friends' twin girls who were all about the same age. A cake, a game, a few balloons, and a couple of presents was all it was. Simple but perfect. Jordan wanted to give Grant a gift, too. He gave him a lollipop and a quarter and put it in an envelope. From Grant's reaction, you would have thought he had given him a million bucks! He was so happy! I have sat through many children's parties and watched as the kid opens present after present with not much more than a quick glance at each gift and then on to the next one. It was refreshing to watch the simplest gifts give him such great joy.

The boys especially loved watching the trash truck come once a week and would run to the front room bay window to observe and talk to each other about how strong the truck's teeth were. They would get very excited when they saw a tow truck or emergency vehicle on the road and were thrilled with impromptu family field trips to the Sheriff's helicopter hangar, the police station, and the fire station.

Their first time going trick-or-treating was lots of fun once they realized what they were supposed to do. They tried on their costumes and practiced knocking and saying, "Trick or treat!" when I opened the door. They had experienced the crèche version of Thanksgiving but they seemed pretty amazed at the size of the bird and the feast laid out in November that first year home. By Christmas they knew English well enough to understand the true meaning of the holiday but not enough to see through the pretend Santa Claus shenanigans we pulled on them.

Taking them to the snow for the first time, setting traps for a mischievous leprechaun, and placing teeth under the pillow for the Tooth Fairy were added to the list of magical memories we created all in that first year. I recorded all these first time experiences in photos and arranged them in a beautiful scrapbook for the boys. Occasionally we flip through that album together and look back wistfully at a time when life was less complicated.

They were very happy most of the time and very loud! They enjoyed playing with the neighbors or friends that would come visit, but mostly with each other. I was so thankful they had each other to go through life with. They were, and still are, the best of friends.

Elizabeth Molina

12
Third-World Kids in the First World

About two months after the boys came home, they were invited to the birthday party of Jordan's classmate from preschool. Our friend's twin daughters were also attending. I didn't think it was a good idea, mostly because I wasn't sure I could handle it. I still wasn't used to having every minute of my day occupied by small demanding people. Since Mario was working, my friend convinced me to bring them and offered to stay with them while I ran to the grocery store. The party was held at a gymnastics studio. I finally agreed, thinking maybe they would play a lot and get tired out. I took them and stayed for a little while then headed off to do my errand. I left them in my friend's able hands, not too worried. The place was enclosed and full of mats so I wasn't afraid they would get hurt. I don't think even the most prepared adoptive parent would have foreseen what ended up happening. It was a Star Wars–themed birthday party. As a surprise for the birthday boy, his older sibling dressed up as Darth Vader. When it was time for him to make his grand entrance, all the kids were seated at a table enjoying their snacks and cake. I was told that my boys looked up and screamed at the top of their lungs! As quickly as they could scramble out of their seats, they ran around the room anxiously looking for another exit to get away from this tall, masked, monstrous looking thing. They had no idea what it was!

When recounting this event to friends and family, many commented that their own children are wary of all the dressed-up characters at Disneyland and would probably have run, too. At three years old–maybe; at six years old–doubtful. Interestingly, *no other kid screamed or ran out of the room at that party*. Even so, the behavior is communicating something different because they have a history which influences those reactions or responses. Often times other parents witness these things or hear about such experiences and, in an effort to ease the new parents' worries, assume that because their child or a friend's child had a similar reaction or experience to what the adoptive child had, that it's no big deal. It is a big deal. My child may be doing it for very different reasons. To say it's no big deal is to dismiss their history, their loss, their pain, their grief, their trauma, their lack of experiences.[1]

The challenges our boys faced may appear to be common themes among children from developed and developing countries. However, the reason behind the behavior is so much more complex, so much more than "all kids do that" or "lots of kids have that problem." Their behaviors are rooted in their individual traumatic history.

Food

The difference in eating was huge when our boys first came home. They would eat twice as much and twice as fast as us. This may have been because they were so conditioned to eating their small meals quickly in the crèche. If a younger child was full but still had food on their plate, it was given to someone who had finished theirs and still wanted more. I grew up in an impoverished situation myself and, as a young child, I was accustomed to not always having food at home. I can remember thinking whenever I had food in front of me, *My next meal might not be as plentiful as this. I'd better eat as much as possible and quickly so I can have seconds before it's all gone.* As a young adult, I recalled having this internal conversation again with myself. Even when I knew I would never go hungry as I did as a child, I would consume much more than I needed to. Old habits die hard. The authors of *The Connected Child* state that "The [food] deprivation [children] suffered early in life has hardwired their primitive brain to believe that starvation is just around the corner."[2] I recognized early on the outward manifestation of this habitual way of thinking that children from extreme poverty develop, as I did myself. The difference though (aside from the drastic situation they were coming from), was that their minds at three and six years of age, with all of their life experiences, could not wrap around the idea that there would be a next meal.

Since our family had doubled in size our grocery bill, understandably, also doubled after the first couple of months. We decided to plant a garden. We had the space and my husband did a good job caring for it. I told him which fruits and vegetables we wanted to eat and he planted them. The boys loved the garden because they could grab a tomato or some grapes off the vine if they were hungry while playing out back. Our hope was that by seeing food growing in the garden and having free access to it, they would feel a greater sense of security. While the boys were accustomed to the concept of growing food to eat, never before did they have to share it with so few. When I asked Jordan what he remembered about his life with his birth parents (prior to the crèche) he recalled having food to eat but it was always picked from the plant or tree. The crèche also had a small garden. Never had they seen or experienced buying food from a grocery store. I think they started to gather, through our grocery shopping and meal preparations (which they curiously watched and even helped with), that the food we grew in the garden was just a small portion of what we ate and was more to complement the food we bought rather than a dire necessity for our subsistence.

I started them on a food schedule when they first came home to help them feel more secure about food. I made them a small poster that showed them when they would have their meals and snacks. We had to constantly redirect them to it at first. Eventually they learned that we would always provide them with enough food to eat. There were still some challenges we faced, like sneaking food. We thought we had escaped that common behavior of malnourished children. We tried to convince the boys it wasn't necessary since food is extremely plentiful here.

One night early in the spring, and soon after the boys had come home from Haiti, my husband had brought in a handful of small ripe tomatoes from the garden and put them on top of the microwave oven in a small dish. It was shortly after dinner and I walked back into the kitchen after bathing the boys. For some reason the tomatoes Mario had picked caught my eye. I looked at them and noticed they weren't sitting quite like a fully rounded tomato would sit, and so I picked one up. I saw a hole in it. Thinking maybe they were all rotten, I picked each one up to examine it closer. I realized that each one had been bitten into and then placed back upside down so they looked like they were still whole. By this time both boys were getting ready for bed. I called my husband into the kitchen to show him and then we called Jordan in (Grant couldn't reach that high yet). While we knew the answer to our question, we were confused because the boys were allowed to pick tomatoes whenever they wanted, we asked anyway in a gentle voice, "Did you bite into all these tomatoes?" He knew he'd been caught but stood there with an innocent look on his sweet little face. When we asked him why he did it he said in his quiet, raspy voice, *"Paske mwen renmen tomat"* (Because I love tomatoes). Still to this day I can't look at a tomato and not think of that little event without drawing a wide smile on my face.

Recently, I was driving and my oldest son started laughing to himself. When I asked him what he was laughing about he told me that he was thinking about when they first came home from Haiti. They would take turns sneaking into the kitchen for food. One day it was Grant's turn, he told me. Grant had come back to their room with dog food! Jordan asked him, "What's that? Why did you bring dog food?" Grant replied, "It was all I could find." Jordan said he didn't eat it but maybe his brother ate some. Some years later I caught Grant eating a dog biscuit as he was carrying the box out to give our dog a treat! I think he was curious about what we were feeding the dog that time, but it's very possible he ate the dog food in their room that night!

The boys' appetite did eventually taper off and then it would increase again with each growth spurt. Today, they both out-eat my husband and I, and yet don't have an ounce of fat on their body. I made sure they didn't have hardly any sugary or high fat foods or beverages when they were really little, and I got them in the habit of playing outdoors *a lot*. I figured that if they were going to sneak food, it would be best to keep the kitchen stocked with healthy food. I made a point of educating them about the food choices available and why we have to eat certain foods. They have learned to recognize when they are full and which foods are sure to fill them and provide them with energy to run and the ability to focus. This all was as much for me as it was for them.

It wasn't all veggies and lean proteins because it's also important to teach balance. That's where the idea of "Sugar Saturday" started. We borrowed this idea from a neighbor and embraced it as our own. I wasn't sure how to monitor their sugar intake during the week (or my own, for that matter!). Anytime they asked for anything with refined sugar we said "Sure, on Sugar Saturday" and Jordan and Grant were satisfied with that answer. I don't think the neighbor's kids bought that answer as readily as our boys. On Saturday they would choose one or two pieces from their Halloween bucket and enjoy it. It became a tradition for my husband to take them to the candy store to pick out something for Sugar Saturday if they were out of their holiday stash.

They were very good about eating everything put in front of them (we served small portions for the first serving) and we taught them to try everything, even the stuff they didn't think they would like. Grant didn't like the taste of vegetables (what kid does?) but he ate a few bites if they were on his plate. These habits were probably not as difficult to develop with our boys, given their background, but it still took work. Today I am thankful I put in the effort to establish good eating habits with them. They are not picky eaters, will try almost anything, and are fairly knowledgeable about what and how much food they should put into their bodies. Children who come from poverty are definitely at a higher risk of developing an over-eating disorder. It is something I struggled with for years and now have to deal with the health consequences of those choices.

The boys would gasp if they saw another kid their age drinking soda. Grant would even take it upon himself to inform them that "Kids are not allowed to drink soda." This happened quite often until they realized it was only me that was imposing these rules on them. They didn't feel tricked though, as I have always explained to the boys my reasons for everything. They enjoy candy and even an occasional soda now that they are a little older. They eventually learned that consuming in moderation and lots of physical activity is key to a well-balanced diet.

Attachment

When they first came home they would yell twice as loud as any other kids. My husband and I were not used to hearing kids yelling in our neighborhood and were afraid our neighbors would complain. They never did, but we were always hushing the boys. I regret that. I wish I had allowed them to be the carefree, spirited kids they were. When a friend came to visit with her Haitian adopted children they would all play together and were even louder. Once, we were visiting other Haitian adopted friends from the crèche while in Utah. We met up with them at a museum. It was a good thing it was a museum for children because the noise level of all of them together was drawing lots of attention. This was just part of the culture established at the orphanage. They are joyful, loud, sociable kids when among each other. The bonds from their early childhood were seamlessly reestablished once they were back together.

    I had them play outside for long hours every day. The first few days they would come in and out the back door every two or three minutes. Sometimes it was just to say, "Hi!" or to ask for a snack. As newbie parents, it drove us crazy! Finally, I locked the back door and said they had to play outside for at least 15 minutes without coming in. We had a sunroom that was all windows and a sliding glass door. The back door was also all glass so I was able to see pretty much the whole backyard, which was gated, and hear easily if there was a problem. This worked okay until one time they decided to 'water' the grass. I changed the rule to allow potty breaks. If I had better educated myself on adoption issues early on, I would have realized that they simply wanted reassurance that we were going to be there for them if they came back inside. Their insecurity could also be due to the fact that they were voluntarily relinquished, regardless of the birth parents reasoning. They were in a new culture, a new place, trying to communicate in a new language. In their short lives they had lived with three sets of caregivers, in two countries. I wish I could go back and handle those early days differently, having the patience and stamina to reassure them with a smile every single time they came running in.

We tried to keep it to just the four of us in the beginning and to limit the visitors. Understandably, many people who had prayed with us through the process or who had followed our journey of adoption were excited to meet our little guys. We had read that it was crucial to the bonding process for our boys to know that we were their primary caregivers and to learn to turn to us to have their physical and emotional needs met. This would allow them to attach to us and establish a foundation on which to grow our intimate relationship as a family. At times it was awkward trying to explain this foreign concept to friends with biological children.

Attachment is something most parents know about and are able to establish from birth (and earlier) with their child. Once the child is old enough to express his or her needs, people assume they are securely attached. They feel as though they are doing the parents a favor by helping to meet this need, whether it be getting the child a cup of water or holding and comforting them when they are crying. Taking our kids out of their arms when they just wanted to love on them was even harder to explain especially when it was our child that had initially jumped into their arms.

The way Grant, in particular, would indiscriminately search out affection with whichever mom-like person who happened to be around was worrisome. He showed signs of attachment distress. Fortunately, we recognized it immediately and took steps right away to relieve his distress and to be the ones to meet his every emotional and physical need. He had only been in the orphanage for a year–right after he had been weaned at two years of age. We could tell that he was attached to his birth parents based on the way he interacted with the father when he came to say goodbye. When he came home with us, he had in his favor his age and ability to attach. This helped him quickly and easily bond with Mario and me. This bonding was crucial to his future emotional and social development.

Jordan had not been living with his birth parents for a while by the time we came along. He was not attached to them as observed by his lack of affection or even physical closeness to his birth father on that last visit. When we did see him with both parents the first time, we saw them at the transit house. He interacted with them in a friendly way but we thought maybe they were people he knew from their village or distant relatives. He did not engage with them like a child would with his parents, especially if he hadn't seen them in a while. This is one of the reasons why we were unsure as to who they were at that first, chance encounter.

Unfortunately Jordan did not attach to us as easily as his brother had. This could have been due to broken bonds early in his development upon placement in the orphanage. Once there, he was cared for by the nannies but not like a mother cares for her child. The orphanage had over 60 children in their care ranging from newborns to five years old. Obviously the younger ones would get the higher ratio of caregivers and the older, more independent ones would mostly self-care with supervision. The ones that could walk would not be held. This lack of consistent affection for over two years, paired with the need to survive and stand up for himself, had manifested in an attachment disorder.

We did not have him professionally evaluated and diagnosed but he does exhibit many of the characteristic behaviors of reactive attachment disorder (RAD).[3] What we have witnessed and struggle with most are his controlling and avoiding behaviors, feelings of entitlement, elusiveness, aloofness, and a lack of affection. Even after seven years, he does not seek out our affection, but at times will be affectionate toward his younger siblings. My hope is for him to be able to reciprocate love in a lasting relationship later in his life.

We made and continue to make extensive attempts to bond and attach with Jordan and have made some progress. I tell him I love him. He tolerates a hug and a kiss now and then but never initiates it and hardly reciprocates it. When we talk about it, he says it's uncomfortable for him to be affectionate with older people. He shows his love in other ways. Often times he brings me a piece of candy from an event he may have attended or he will pick my favorite flower while he is out walking the dog and bring it home to me.

Brain Development and Learning Issues

The boys were very creative in their play and played twice as hard as any other kids. They would draw almost life-size pictures of helicopters or airplanes on the cement with chalk and then pretend to ride in them. Jordan would take their toy truck or go-kart and pack it up with other toys then stop and pick up Grant, who would ride on the back, mimicking a Haitian *tap-tap*. They would spend hours playing with their toy trains and cars and trucks and motorcycles. When the big earthquake happened in Haiti on January 12, 2010, I had the news blaring from the TV all day long. The boys watched, too, as they played with their planes and trucks and would re-enact taking loads of food or money to the Haitian people. I should have been suspicious when Grant was piling dry dog food pebbles into his tow trucks!

The boys did not lack any imagination. They appeared to have a normal range of intelligence when I observed them in their school setting at the crèche. My teaching experience told me that learning issues can manifest at any time. That fall we enrolled Jordan in Kindergarten at a private school. He enjoyed the social aspect of it, was well behaved, respectful, hardworking, and well liked. He was reserved but enjoyed playing with some of the other kids. As a trained teacher, I was able to identify his academic struggles early on. Memory work was and still is one of his biggest obstacles with school. An average student needs 25 to 50 repetitions for information to become stored permanently in their long term memory. Jordan needed 200 or more repetitions and still, if the item was not retrieved regularly, he would have to relearn it all again. For example, in third grade he was assigned with memorizing the multiplication facts. Now, in seventh grade—four years later—he has most of them memorized. However, if I allow him to take the whole summer off from just reviewing them, he may regress on more than half of the facts.

Grant's memory seemed to be just fine. However, once he started school he showed signs of dyslexia. This is a result of the brain incorrectly interpreting the information it is receiving. It can be visual or auditory reversals which means he flips some of the numbers and letter sounds. For example, he will say or write 11 but mean 12 and vice versa. The most problematic letter sounds for him are the short *e* and *i* vowels. He seems to hear them as the same sound and will guess if he hasn't memorized which one is the correct spelling.

Since I began noticing a consistent pattern in the errors he was making, I correct and gently remind him that his brain likes to trick him and he needs to double check his work to be sure he has written or said what he means. He has made huge improvements and rarely gets "tricked" anymore. He also had a hard time learning to read but has greatly improved in the last two years. He reads out loud to me for 30 minutes twice a day. This allows me to monitor the types of errors he makes and his progress. It teaches him to self-monitor and to be mindful, which increases his comprehension.

These learning issues may be attributed mainly to their lack of proper nutrition and stimulation in the early years when their brains were developing. It makes sense that Grant's issues are not as severe as Jordan's because he was only three years old when he came home to us. Once he began receiving the proper nourishment and stimulation, his brain development got on track. Jordan was six years old by the time he came home. He has made tremendous growth but is still not quite at grade level in subjects that require rote memorization skills. We are now seeing the benefits of starting him in school a year later. He is experiencing success which boosts his self-confidence and motivates him to continue trying.

Although I recognized that they were struggling shortly after each entered school, we decided not to have the boys formally tested or diagnosed. As a former public school teacher, I saw many children with learning issues diagnosed and then placed in either special education, resource class, reading intervention, or some other type of remediation program. Based on test scores, observations, and other formal assessments, the regular classroom teacher would recommend students to a student study team. This team, usually comprised of the teacher, principal, school psychologist, and parent, would meet periodically and would put together an action plan and then monitor the student's progress. This would hopefully lead the child to succeed academically or at least progress in that direction.

For better or for worse, this meant that the child was then labeled accordingly on the school cumulative record. As a teacher, I see the value in knowing what you are up against, but I also know the pitfalls of labels. As a parent, the disadvantages of labeling far outweighed the benefits. Consequently, we decided to forgo testing. I myself was an elementary reading remediation teacher for a few years as well as a regular classroom teacher for many years. Students who were below grade level, but didn't qualify for other interventions, would come to me during the regular school day for small group learning. For a number of students, this provided that extra bit of attention they needed in order to get them over the hurdle they were struggling to clear. I watched many students progress because of the extra help they received; unfortunately, I also saw many fail. It could be because they were either misdiagnosed and/or labeled as having a learning disability (self-fulfilling prophecy) or they had a more severe learning disability and it was not adequately dealt with because they didn't qualify under the minimum guidelines. In my observation, this negatively affected their self-esteem, which was heartbreaking.

A good friend of mine is a psychologist. Her primary focus is testing and the differential diagnosis of learning disabilities. I respect her, value her opinion, and appreciate her candidness. When I asked her what would result from having my boys tested and diagnosed (which she recommended), she said that I would then be able to make an informed decision on whether to seek out intervention. This seemed harmless enough, even helpful. However, I was afraid of the label and its repercussions. The reality is that if a trained teacher works one-to-one with a student, the struggles are easily identifiable and the intervention strategies are equally accessible, especially with the resources we now have available online. I knew my kids better than anyone. I knew what their weaknesses and strengths were. Her answer to my next question was very important. I asked, "What would that treatment look like?" She replied, "Probably one-to-one academic tutoring by a trained professional tailored to their specific learning deficiencies." I replied, "You mean like a personal teacher that knows how to address their specific learning problems?"

That year we began homeschooling. Jordan was

entering his third grade year. Second grade was a total wash for him. He was way too interested in all the fun the kids around him were having and consequently never got any work done. I figured that if he was going to come home with piles of work to do I might as well just school him at home and save a buck. The second grade teacher had also expressed that she felt we should consider having him tested for ADD and possibly be medicated. There were many things that should have been different about that year and potentially would have produced a different outcome; we did not believe medication to be one of them. The traditional model classroom didn't work for Jordan. Either way, he had even more catching up to do now and the learning gap was affecting his self-esteem.

Grant stayed in school another year. Mid-year, he was invited to be part of a reading club that stayed after school a couple of days a week. I appreciated the extra help he was given and it reaffirmed to me the value in small group learning. I couldn't see them playing catch up all through elementary school, being labeled, or feeling like a failure. Seeing the success Jordan had at home, we decided that I would homeschool both of them the following year.

Once I realized that my boys' best chance was having their own private teacher to help them realize their fullest potential, I thought, "Who better than the person that loves them the most and has the greatest motivation to see them succeed?" There are many homeschool naysayers that wigged out and immediately thought I was crazy to do it, that my kids would be weird and unsocialized, and so on. I figured that between sports practice twice a week, Sunday school, Bible study, and co-op once a week, we had the socializing down. Socializing with kids their age was not high on the priority list of school time activities, especially when they were struggling with learning to read, write, and do math. They socialized after school. I think that traditional school is a good choice for the traditional student. That approach to education does not work for every single child. I was not willing to wait and see if it worked for my boys.

Medical Issues

I am thankful that the boys did not have any major medical issues to deal with when they came home. There was of course the issue of parasites. The most unpleasant part of that was collecting the stool samples. Jordan was a quick fix with one or two samples but Grant had a few gastrointestinal issues to deal with so we felt like we were scooping for weeks! When I say *we*, I mean Mario. He was the hero when it came to collecting the samples.

The boys were both diagnosed with *Entamoeba histolytica*. Additionally, Grant had *Giardia lamblia*. Both are intestinal parasitic infections that cause diarrhea and other gastrointestinal problems. These parasites are protozoa (single-celled organisms that only divide within the host) and enter the body in cyst form. Once in the small intestine, the cyst will divide into two trophozoites, which then multiply and remain in the small intestine until they are getting ready to exit the colon—thus the poop test.

They are both contracted through contaminated water or food, and *Giardia* is commonly ingested through fecal-contaminated materials. This makes sense that Grant, who was only a toddler and just beginning to be potty-trained, would have *Giardia* and not Jordan. He was probably just learning about proper sanitation at the crèche. With 60 to 70 children, it can be difficult for caregivers to make sure they all wipe correctly or wash their hands well. I had a difficult time teaching just two boys about proper sanitation once they came home. During one visit, I kept reminding Grant not to put non-food items in his mouth. With lots of little hands touching everything, I could only imagine the germs. He responded every time in the sweetest little worried voice, *"Paske li gen mikwob? Nou ka mouri?"* (Because it has germs? And we can die?). The onsite preschool teacher assured me he was teaching them proper sanitation. Once home, I would remind them every time I heard them exiting the bathroom to wash their hands with soap but, as an extra measure of caution, I would follow their path with disinfecting wipes.

Because *Giardia* is a hardy, contagious parasite lasting months in cold water, a red flag went up. The pediatrician was obligated to report the case. We were treated to an extensive phone interview with the County Public Health. The fear of diseases spreading is real and not to be taken lightly in any country. I was happy to cooperate with the nurse on the phone but, living in a developed country, I can see how it can be ostracizing.

It is easy here in the US to give medication and be done with it, if it even is a problem. In Haiti, the reinfection cycle repeats over and over due to the lack of medication, education, or proper hygiene and, for many, the absence of modern toilets or safe disposal of waste.

The symptoms the boys displayed were loose stools, stomach cramps, and flatulence. They also had distended bellies. This can be a sign of malnutrition due to an infestation of parasitic worms. As a result of the worms, there can be a vitamin A deficiency, inflammation of the intestines, and possible weight loss. The treatments for all of these are similar and it could have been a case of killing two birds with one stone. Fortunately, a course of an antibiotic, metronidazole, fixed the boys intestinal issues quite easily. About six months after they had been home their bellies appeared normal.

Grant also had a really bad case of what we thought was halitosis for several years after coming home. We were vigilant with his oral care and yet at his cleaning every six months the dentist would scold me for not taking better care of his dental hygiene. The odor was fecal which is indicative of a bowel obstruction. It turned out he had *Helicobacter pylori* which is a common bacteria causing an infection in the digestive tract. It can also cause gastritis or gastroesophageal reflux disease symptoms and abdominal pain, which Grant also experienced. The triple therapy treatment his pediatrician prescribed for 14 days knocked it out easily.

Behavior Issues

Looking back, I can say that the boys did not exhibit any notable negative behavior issues. At the time, I may have assessed the situation differently. I didn't have a high tolerance for loud, rambunctious boys. Fortunately, with the passing of time comes the changing of perspective. I realize now that they were just active boys! Sadly, that was not the case with some of the others that were adopted from the crèche, I came to find out. That's not the case for many other parents who have adopted internationally. Some faced extreme cases of reactive attachment disorder and had to institutionalize their child for the safety of others in their home, as well as to help the child learn to cope with their issues. Of course, we never know what issues we may have to deal with in our own biological children.

  I will say that my boys were loud, energetic kids that did lots of things out of curiosity and without really thinking about the consequences. Not always having a point of reference, they often appeared to lack common sense to those unfamiliar with their unique background. The major differences between them and other kids their age were the sheer number of incidents and the kinds of things they were curious about. One day, while working on an assignment for homeschool, Jordan wrote about a time he was investigating in the chicken coop. He was curious about where the chicken eggs were coming from. He knew the chickens were laying them as we had sat a couple of times and watched them lay in the nesting boxes. He was curious specifically about the orifice the egg was coming out of. One day while collecting the eggs, he decided to pick up the chicken and take a closer, hands-on approach to his investigation. I'm sure the chicken didn't appreciate this as much as I did that day in homeschool. The story is one I have kept in his writing portfolio mostly as a reminder of his sillier, carefree days.

 There are days when my boys act like they deserve whatever gadget every other kid has and then I gently remind them that they didn't have so much before they came to live with us and that their own siblings in Haiti still don't have all that we have. Then they are okay with not having all the latest and greatest material things. I think it is important to keep them grounded and to remember where we came from and that none of us are deserving but have what we have by the grace of God–just because He loves us. I read the following on Facebook recently: A rich person is not one who has the most, but is the one who needs the least. My hope is that my boys grow up to have very rich lives.

13
A Baby Sister?

Although I certainly had my hands full with two loud, rowdy, full-of-life boys, I was still curious what it would be like to raise a girl...to have a daughter. Maybe we are born with this narcissistic inclination to have a little mini-me. Maybe it was Grant's constant desire for a baby sister. Tired of being the youngest, he continually reminded me that a little sister would be good for him to teach (or boss around, depending on how you looked at it). He wouldn't let up about it. He asked and very often included this request in our night time family prayers. I would jokingly say to my family, "There's too much testosterone in this house! We need a girl to counterbalance it." Whatever it was, the desire was growing.

About four years had passed since we had adopted

the boys. Life was starting to feel easier, more comfortable. The boys were well adapted to our family life and routines. They were mostly caught up with their chronological age in their behavior, language, and emotions. They were more independent. There were still some challenges academically, but they had made tremendous progress and I felt confident that in the large scheme of things they would be just fine. Although we were still homeschooling—which is a full-time job in and of itself—and there were days when the boys' energy levels were enough to make me cry, I began to imagine having a baby girl.

    By now I was completely at peace with the idea of never birthing a child. Maybe even a tiny bit thankful that it wasn't in God's plan? I have a hard enough time managing just a simple cold or flu; I couldn't imagine what it would be like going through nine months of feeling sick, bloated, and overly emotional. Given my history, I am sure it would have been a difficult pregnancy even if we had explored more fertility treatments and actually conceived. Mario didn't want to adopt internationally again because of the cost and the wait. I didn't want to go through the foster care system because I wasn't sure I could handle it. The old fears began to creep back into my mind.

    I hadn't seen my friend since Jordan and her son were in Kindergarten. I knew she had started fostering a baby girl shortly after that, but then we lost touch. Then one day, there it was in my inbox, an email from her.

We reconnected on the phone and I found she had not only adopted two beautiful girls but was also heavily involved in foster care support. The speaker she had lined up for a quarterly Adoption Story Night had to cancel and would I like to come speak that Friday at her event? I planned to speak that night but I did not plan on what was laid on my heart afterwards.

I was pleasantly surprised when she asked me to share our family story. The number one response we hear when we tell others we adopted our boys from Haiti is, "God bless you for doing that!" These well-meaning folks tend to see *us* as some kind of saviors to poor helpless children. That is not the case. While we do recognize the very important need for us to follow the gospel in "defending the cause of the fatherless" (Isaiah 1:17) and to "look after the orphans and widows" (James 1:27), we didn't feel like adopting our kids was this noble thing we did for them. It was just the way we felt led to build our family. Mario and I have always seen the boys as such a blessing *to us*. Our inability to conceive could have left us childless. Adoption was a huge gift to us! I don't believe God always planned for us to adopt the boys–I believe His plan was for them to be raised by their birth parents. But I do believe He led us to them knowing they would be relinquished. God took a situation that was difficult and used it for good. God can use anyone he wants to accomplish His purpose, but those that are obedient are the ones most blessed.

I really enjoyed the informal setting of Adoption Story Night, sharing our international adoption journey, and answering the questions that followed. It was then, as I walked the eager faces in her living room through our adoption journey, that I realized that there was a more relevant reason for God building our family this way; just like the blind man that Jesus healed in the Bible. He wasn't born blind as a punishment to his parents or himself as a result of sin. He was simply born blind, and in his healing God would be glorified. The boys' birth parents had their own reasons for giving up their children to adoption. God certainly wasn't punishing us for our sins by not giving us biological kids. God chose us to adopt our beautiful sons, that *He would be credited.* This was not the first time I had shared all the ways God met us along in our journey. It was at this time, however, that I saw the true reason for those moments we had the privilege to experience; that we might bring glory to God in sharing His perfect design for our family.

After I shared, another couple shared their adoption story. The lady, who is now a friend, shared her similar experience with infertility. Her painful words touched my heart as I remembered that part of my own journey. She eventually was able to birth a daughter but felt the Lord had more children planned for their family. As a slightly older couple, biological children were no longer an option. They became involved in foster care and eventually adopted their second daughter. This had opened their eyes and hearts to the world of adoption through foster care. I was really impressed with this couple's ability to allow God to lead them in building their family in this way. This was a road I had been too afraid to consider. Since then, they have recently added two more girls to their family. It has not always been an easy road for them, having their hearts broken more than once in placements that did not end in adoption. They have been faithful to God in serving Him by caring for the most vulnerable of His children.

I recall talking with my friend and another mom afterwards about their foster-to-adopt (also called fost-adopt) experience. They were brutally honest and shared not only the good parts but also the challenging, heartbreaking parts. I remember the physical feeling of God warming my heart to the idea that night! It was a mixed feeling of excitement, fear, and anticipation of what God had planned for us. The same fears I had four years earlier were still there. But this time I knew that if God was for it then He would walk me through the process, helping me to overcome those fears along the way.

I prayed all the way home from the event that night. I wanted to be sure it was God leading and that it was not just the desire of my flesh to have a little girl. I laid my request before the Lord: If God wanted us to pursue it then my husband would have to be open to it. I knew God would be faithful in speaking through Mario as he had many times before and I was confident

He would give me an answer either way. When I got home that evening and told Mario that I wanted us to pray about it and consider it, he didn't miss a beat. He just said, "Sure, let's do it!"

Initially, I didn't share Mario's confidence in my ability to handle it all even though my heart wanted to go for it. However, if there was someone to hold my hand each step of the way, and I was surrounded by so many others who had done it and made it through, I now was willing to walk this road in faith. Since those first steps into the adoption world, I have realized that there is this huge community of support and resources. My friend has established a whole ministry for fost-adopt families that includes a love closet; Bible study and weekly support group; networking opportunities for foster moms and kids; a private Facebook group to allow foster moms to vent, share, pray for their specific cases; and ongoing training for foster parents. There are numerous other nonprofit groups that partner with the county and foster family agencies to support the foster parents. These range from providing respite by a licensed caregiver to personal bonding and attachment counseling. Even if someone doesn't feel led to take on foster care personally, there is a whole array of ways to help and support foster children and foster families. My education in fost-adopt was just starting.

I reflected on my biggest fear as I prayed and pondered God's will for our family. That fear was getting my heart broken. How could I love a child like my own (because that's what you do) and then have her taken from me. That is probably the number one reason that many people won't even consider foster care and why many Christians are not obedient to the call to care for the orphans in this way. When we started our adoption with the boys, I knew that once we were matched, they were ours. I knew it might take years to finally bring them home, but once they were home I knew it was final. At that time my heart understood that we have our children and nobody can take them from us. This helped me to be more open to the risks I would have to take in this next adoption journey we were about to embark on.

The amount of time our hearts would be invested in foster care was still disquieting. We had heard stories of friends of friends waiting years to adopt, all the while caring for, loving, bonding with, and nurturing kids that they believed would be legally theirs only to wake up one day and have to give them back. This is seen all the time in the media. We knew this could happen to us. What we eventually learned over time is that it isn't about us, or protecting our hearts. It's about loving sacrificially for the well-being of another.

The foster care system and its methods are flawed for sure, but at the core is the preservation of the biological family unit. After watching my son shed a tear as his Haitian father walked out the door, my heart was crushed for him. I can appreciate how important blood ties are. I learned that every child wants to know where they came from. My youngest son Grant said to me one day when he was about six years old, "Tell me again how we got here." Fortunately, I had educated myself on this topic as I waited to bring them home. I learned that it is important to either make a Lifebook that shows in pictures where they came from and how they came to be a part of the new family or at the very least to retell the story to the child often, adding in more details as they are ready to hear them. We had begun this storytelling from the beginning with the boys. We chose to be honest and open with them about their biological family and to pray for them. Many adoptees search out their biological parents once they are adults because they want to know, "Who do I look like? What is my history? How did I lose my biological family?" Preserving these biological ties is a good thing for the adoptee as long as the child is safe, nurtured, cared for, and well loved. Sadly, this is not always the case and that is when the ties must be severed and a closed adoption becomes necessary.

 The vetting process for foster care was one I could not imagine going through again. The mountains of paperwork to gather did not sound like a whole lot of fun to me. It is a thorough process to say the least, and with good reason. It's absurd to take a child from a bad situation to an even worse one. Besides the obvious case of child trafficking, there are many cases of abuse and neglect that occur within the foster care system. Although the training and paperwork was overwhelming, it seemed a small sacrifice to make in exchange for a human being that I would one day call my daughter.

The idea of getting "damaged goods" is another reason why many people will not choose fost-adopt as a viable option for building a family. As a teacher and police officer, we were all too familiar with many children labeled as such. Mario had seen foster kids on the streets while working patrol and I had watched them slip through the cracks working in certain public schools. This same callous thought went through our minds when we first contemplated adopting. The funny thing is, there are no guarantees with how even biological children will turn out. Children who have been abused, neglected, or abandoned are not at fault for their misfortune. They should not have to bear the punishment for the decisions of their parents. They deserve a family, someone to love them, to care for them, and to help them be the best version of themselves. Fortunately, I learned to see them as God sees them: as precious children.

But, I was not yet on the same page as God. I wanted to build my family. God wanted me to care for his children when they were most vulnerable. I knew I couldn't have one without the other but I was still trying to go into it assuming the least amount of risk to my heart. I even told the social worker, "I'm not doing this for lofty or noble reasons. I just want to add to my family." She smiled a knowing kind of smile—the kind you put on when you know that there is a bigger and better plan but you have to let the other person discover it on their own. It was like she knew God would change my heart and mold it to His will through the whole process. Fortunately, this statement didn't cause her to drop our case altogether. She knew my husband's view, too, which was, "Yes, we would like to adopt, but if we can help out some kids with a safe place to stay until that opportunity presents itself, even better." My husband is much more sensitive and compassionate than I am, and it is in his nature to care for vulnerable animals and children. It's what he does.

Although I was still not entirely comfortable with the idea of fost-adopt, I have since learned that God never lets us be completely comfortable. It's not what He planned for our time here on earth. He means for us to be slightly uncomfortable—just enough for us to strive for something better. We need to strive for the goal, heaven, a perfect paradise with Him. The journey here on earth is merely a chance for us (His creation) to be molded by Him (our Creator) into the best version of ourselves. We will be this "best version" in heaven for eternity with Jesus. I wasn't there yet. My heart and my flesh were not seeing things the same way, but I was willing to let God lead me. I know now that in time, He would mold my heart and mind so that I would be able to accomplish His purpose and will.

14
Starting Over Again

We began the paperwork with a foster family agency (FFA) in early 2013 and signed up for the training sessions. The trainings were intense and the vetting process was scrutinizing. The paperwork this time was not as cumbersome as the first time around with international adoption but still we had to apply, have background checks completed, and submit financial documents, letters of recommendation, doctor's reports, and more. The home study was also required just as in international adoption. They delved deep into our history as children and parents, more so than with the first home study. The FFA held training classes and were very thorough. Aside from the obligatory CPR and First Aid course, we covered topics that included basic child development; communication; dealing with separation, loss, and grief; connecting with and correcting the child; and standards and documentation of everything. We attended trainings together on the evenings Mario wasn't working and over some weekends. Each class was four to six hours long. We learned a lot and were thankful we were not heading into this new process blindly. With international adoption, this training is not mandatory but researching and preparing yourself is highly recommended. We met quite a few other couples that were also preparing to become foster parents. We maintained contact with many of them so as to build a community of support.

By May of 2013 we had completed all of our paperwork, training, and home study interviews. We were on our way to becoming certified foster parents licensed under our agency, with the goal to adopt. The only thing left to do was the home study report, and that was to be completed by the FFA. Despite all of it, we still had no clue what to expect next.

The next day we got a call. Could we take over foster care of twin girls that were just 12 months old and could we pick them up in 24 hours? The foster mom who originally accepted them the month prior was overwhelmed with another placement she had and they needed to transfer care to someone else. The FFA is usually called when it is a hardship case and the county is unable to place the kids with a county licensed foster family. This can be when it is a child with special needs, a sibling set, or if they just don't have any county families with openings. The local emergency shelter care facility, which is a non-profit organization, is usually a last resort. We didn't even have our home study report written! Fortunately, with foster care, a simplified version of the home study can be written up in a matter of hours. This allowed us to take the placement of the twins. The full home study report would have to be completed before we could be identified as potential adoptive parents.

Things moved really quickly after that. I texted my husband first, "Twin baby girls! We pick up TOMORROW!" I knew he had to qualify that day at the sheriff's shooting range and so his phone ringer would be off. Normally, I would just wait for him to return my text or call me, but this was pressing. I knew his vote to accept the placement would be based on whether I thought I could handle the babies, since I would be the one mostly caring for them. I still needed to know he was okay with it before I was able to take the placement. I tried his office and they called the range for me. He got the message and finally called me.

By then I had already called my friend who had introduced me to the whole world of fost-adopt. "We are picking up twin babies tomorrow! I don't have car seats, strollers, or even another crib!" I blurted out to her all in one breath. "Ok, just breathe, Elizabeth. We'll get you everything you need," she reassured me. She put a notice on her Facebook support group for foster parents and within an hour we had another crib, two car seats, and a double stroller. We also needed a different car. We could cram four people and two car seats into our truck but it would be very tight. My CRV didn't even have six seats! Mario took care of that problem shortly after we brought the twins home. Within days I was a minivan-driving mom of four.

Then I called another dear friend who is a mom of twin girls. Hers were toddlers and so the knowledge was still fresh in her mind. When I say she was a godsend, I feel like God physically sent her to help me that very night. I didn't have a clue how to begin making a list of things we would need. She offered to make that list and to go shopping with me that evening. I knew they probably still wore diapers but I had no idea if they would still be on formula or milk and how much milk at a year old? She quickly put another list together of foods I would need and a schedule I should get the babies on. I had never cared fulltime for an infant. Our foster babies were about 13 months old. Sure, I had held infants and had babysat, but mostly toddlers or older kids. I didn't even work in the baby section of Sunday school. I could follow directions, but these baby girls weren't coming with directions. Honestly, without these two friends to guide me early on, I probably would have called the agency back and said, "Sorry, I don't think I can handle the placement."

Mario and I met the twins at the county office the next day and fell in love immediately. I knew there was no going back now. I was captivated by their innocence and cuteness. They were fraternal twins. The smaller petite one with dark hair ("Marisol") was already walking but seemed more reserved than her sister. The taller one with sandy brown hair ("Maricela") made her wants and needs known to anyone who would listen. The boys were just as enthralled with them as we were. They stepped up and became caring, loving big brothers. After completing the necessary paperwork, all six of us headed home.

Mario didn't take as much time off initially as he had when the boys came home. I prayed for that natural mommy instinct to kick in. It did, but mostly I had a lot of help. In the beginning, my sister (who had successfully raised three boys on her own) would come over a couple times a week to help me out with them. I often called my friend with the other twin girls for advice or just to cry from exhaustion. The neighbor at the end of the block (who also had twin baby girls) must have felt really sorry for me because she loaned me her nanny once! I learned their pooping schedule, to have food prepared ahead of time so they didn't have to wait in their high chairs, and to cut food into very small pieces so they wouldn't choke.

Double duty was an understatement! The day would begin early with morning bottles, diaper changes, breakfast, mess clean ups, dressing, and a little time to play with them. Then it was time for diaper changes again, a snack, a walk in the stroller or outside playtime, and lunch. After putting them down for a nap with a clean diaper and a bottle, I had a small amount of time to clean up the mess and do a few chores or take a short nap. Often times, I succumbed to the nap. After they woke up from naps, they would need a diaper change again, another snack, and some more playtime. Seven o'clock could not come quick enough each night. After dinner, I began the evening routine of baths, bottles, and bed as early as I could. I fell into bed each night exhausted, but with a full heart.

In addition to the daily care, foster parents are also the child's advocate. We take them to doctor appointments, refer them for any special needs, line up any services of which they are in need, and make them available for home visits by social workers, therapists, etc. Some weeks we would have a doctor appointment, two social worker visits, and therapy. The twins were somewhat small and not exactly in the optimal range of development for their age. This could have been due to some neglect. They were referred for speech therapy. The therapist would come out to our house once a week and work on developing their vocabulary through play therapy. This was a huge help not only getting their speech development on track but also it gave me an hour to catch up on something.

Documentation was huge. Personal property logs, medication logs, doctor appointment logs, and doctor and dental visit forms had to be filled out and faxed to all social workers; every last bump or scrape, dime-size or larger, had to be documented. It got to the point where I would take a picture and have my FFA social worker screen it and tell me if it was report-worthy before doing the paperwork.

My husband and boys probably felt neglected a little that first month. Luckily it was summer and the boys were quite self-sufficient. It wasn't easy for me to go out of the house with four kids other than for a walk around the block, so we mostly stayed home. There weren't any kids close in age to the boys (7 and 10 years at the time), living on our street. The closest one was a little girl who was about four years old. Often her mom would hang outside with her and her baby brother doing fun things like sidewalk chalk, bubbles, and such. One day, during that first month in which we were all adjusting to life with the babies, Grant walked over to chat with this little girl and her mommy. They had a Slip 'N Slide out front but weren't playing on it yet. A couple of minutes later, Grant walked back home and told me he wanted to take his Slip 'N Slide over to this neighbor's front yard to play with them. The mom had told him that when she put her baby down for a nap at one o'clock he could come back and play on the Slip 'N Slides with the daughter. Every 15 minutes he would either ask me or trot over to the lady and ask her if it was one o'clock yet. He did this for THREE hours!

The county process is a confusing one to understand. When children are removed from the home for the first time, birth parents are given a court date. Depending on the reasons for removal, which can vary from physical or sexual abuse to neglect and child endangerment, the judge may give them six months or more to rehabilitate. During this time, their children are placed in kinship care (care by a qualified relative) or with a foster family. The county may or may not offer to pay for the rehabilitation services. If they complete all the requirements, they are usually reunified with their children at the end of the designated period of time. We were told that the twins were going to be reunified with their birth parents as they had been offered services for rehabilitation. We knew from the beginning that these beautiful girls would not be our forever daughters. Even so, it didn't make it any easier and I couldn't stop myself from loving them as though they would be. The goal of foster care is to preserve the biological family unit. My head knew this was the best plan, if at all possible. My heart wasn't convinced.

Throughout the time of placement, the familial bond is maintained by weekly supervised visits with the birth parents. Aside from maintaining the relationship, it also gives the birth parents the chance to care for their children. Hopefully, this one-hour-a-week visit motivates them to complete the court imposed requirements. The foster parent can choose to meet the birth parents in person or coordinate with a county liaison to handle the drop-off and pick-up of the visits. Not really knowing what to expect, we chose to keep our identity confidential initially and used the county liaison. That first time I had to drop off the twins at the county office for a visit with their birth parents, I found myself feeling protective and angry with people I had never met, in a situation of which the details I hardly knew. I wanted to punish these people for not taking care of their precious daughters, especially when there are so many women (like myself) who are unable to have biological children and would love to raise them. In that moment, it was all about me, my feelings, my history. My attitude was not Christ-like. Who was I to say I was more deserving of these babies than their biological parents? The truth is that none of us are deserving. Only by the grace of God are we entrusted with our precious babies, and each of them only for a period of time.

My friend who had walked this road years before me was ready and waiting with a wealth of knowledge and experience and an understanding heart. After empathizing with me, the first (and best) piece of advice she gave me was to let the birth parents see the love of Christ in me through my caring for their daughters without judging them. "Go alongside them and encourage them to complete the rehabilitation process so that they can be entrusted with their kids again, and so that they will learn to do it well," she said. God began to change my heart through that conversation. The next day I began a communication journal through which I could relate with the birth parents. I tried to keep it simple and to the point. *This is what the girls are eating, learning, doing. We are praying for you.*

The birth parents wrote back a long note every time. They were so thankful that their girls were in safe, caring hands and they were trying their hardest to comply with the courts so they could be reunified. This notebook went back and forth for the next six months. Every time the book came back there were words of gratitude for our support and care of their babies. God began to soften my heart to them and their situation. He opened my eyes little by little and I began to see them the way He sees them—as parents who truly do love their babies and want to do right by them.

Later, I encouraged them to keep the notebook and to look back in it so that they could care for their daughters in a similar manner. Among the many struggles that some birth parents deal with is the lack of education on how to care well for their children. Although I had a way to go on the learning curve, too, I could recognize and admit when I needed help or didn't know something. I had the ability to seek out available resources and the wisdom to distinguish what is in the best interest of the child. Many birth parents that are falling into the system are uneducated in this sense. Along with their own personal inner or behavioral struggles are the struggles to survive and to care well for their children.

After the six-month mark the court moved to unsupervised visits, but I still had not met the birth parents in person. I was still unsure how I would deal with it. In fact, I ran every scenario past the social worker I could think of that would allow me to not have to do the drop-off and pick-up of the twins myself. I was afraid I would resume the earlier bad attitude and I was afraid of what could happen if confidentiality was broken. There was no way around it. Because we were licensed through an agency, we were required to handle the unsupervised visits ourselves. It was inevitable. We would meet the birth parents.

The glimpses of their reality that my police officer husband occasionally reminded me of got the best of my imagination. While I was waiting for them to show up for the first unsupervised visit, which we had arranged to be at the mall, I was scared, nervous, and unsure as to what I would face. I had grown up in a rough neighborhood surrounded by every kind of crime imaginable. Once I left the 'hood, I never looked back. The people approaching me, overjoyed at the sight of their babies, were nothing close to how I had imagined them. Instead of seeing them as undeserving, bad parents, I was able to see them as just people with problems, like everyone in this world. Their issues had more serious consequences as they involved young, vulnerable lives, but they were learning to not succumb to those problems and how to care for their children.

After a couple of unsupervised visits, I felt God leading me to take a risk, to invest myself more into this relationship, if not for my peace of mind then, at a minimum, for the twins' sake. I knew it would be getting closer to the time they would be reunified. I wanted to know that they were going to be okay. I wanted the twins to know that I wanted the best for them, too. Their young minds would only minimally comprehend this through the interactions I would have with their birth parents. I worked up the nerve after a visit to invite their birth parents to go have lunch. I firmly believe the relationship and trust that was established through the communication journal was a vital part of the process. The birth parents had to know and trust me in order to share their story with me. They agreed and so we went to a nearby restaurant and shared a meal. My boys watched the twins in the kiddie play structure while we sat and talked. They shared their struggles with me, how they were doing up to that point, and what their hopes were for their family. I had the opportunity to pray with them for their healing and for their family. That day, God allowed me to see His greater purpose in our doing foster care.

Soon after that, the twins were going on overnight visits with their birth parents. Leaving them that first time was difficult. The situation they were going back to was less than ideal. I can say the county standards are not very high. Their social workers are also overloaded with cases and quite possibly they are grossly underpaid. I trusted God to keep the twins safe but I was not naive to the ways of Satan. I knew that even the things I struggle with take time and work to change and that it is easy to fall back into the same bad habits. It was how I had imagined I would feel when we came to this juncture in the process, but that foreknowledge didn't make it any easier. Sleeping in a quiet house that first night, not knowing if the twins were warm, fed, and safe, was possibly one of the hardest parts. All I could think of was how would I be able to handle the pain I was feeling once they were back with their birth parents for good? I was reminded by the Almighty that this wasn't about me. I thought about how the birth parents must have felt when their babies were taken from them and they didn't have any idea where they were going to be that first night they lost custody.

The twins were eventually reunified with their birth parents. Having to give them up for good was unfathomable. I knew that this part of the adoption journey would be almost unbearable and that I, in my weak flesh, would not be able to handle it gracefully. I knew this about myself since the time my husband and I first considered adoption. God knew as well. I believe his plan was to get me to a place where I utterly and completely depended on Him. In doing so, I would not fold under the pain. I prayed for God to cover me in His grace and allow me to get through the reunification of the twins to their birth parents without too many tears. In the end, I was distracted by a major tooth infection!

A couple nights before we were going to drop off the girls for good with their birth parents, I developed the worst toothache ever. I couldn't sleep, eat, or do much of anything. I was trying to hold off going to the dentist until the twins were back with their birth parents that weekend. I was in so much pain by Friday night that when we went to drop off the twins the next morning, we didn't linger. The tears flowing were more due to the overwhelming pain from my tooth. We unbuckled them, got them out of the van as quick as we could, unloaded all their belongings, and quickly explained that we were heading over to the dentist. I ended up having emergency dental surgery that day! Needless to say, I was completely distracted and the physical pain completely overshadowed the emotional pain; well, at least for that day.

15
Broken Heart

When I was finally awake long enough from the pain medication the oral surgeon had given me, I remembered the girls were gone. It hurt as badly as I imagined it would—so much so that I wanted to quit fostering. My tooth was healing but my heart was broken. Why did I knowingly put myself in such a vulnerable position? Once again my friend was there to talk, to listen to me, and to pray me through it. She reminded me how vulnerable my precious twins were when they came into our care, how God used my family to provide them respite, how much they blossomed while with us, and how it is never really about us.

Mario and I decided that I would take a month off before taking another placement. I wanted to use the time to pray for God's direction for our family. My compassionate and perceptive husband bought me a ticket to Hawaii to visit my brother and his family and some of my dearest friends, including my best friend. I knew if anyone could help me see God's will through the fog of pain I was feeling, it would be her. I planned on leaving for Oahu shortly after my tooth was healed and the oral surgeon signed off on it.

In the days after the twins were gone the house seemed unusually quiet. The boys were not as rambunctious as I had remembered them prior to the twins coming into our life. Compared to having two toddlers running around, they were like quiet little mice. It seemed like they grew up overnight. They voiced their feelings of missing the girls, as did my husband. We all coped with it in different ways. For me, the pain ebbed and flowed. Knowing my boys were permanently mine though, helped. I knew I could hold tightly to them and nobody could take them from me. Some days were harder than others with nothing really to ease the pain. This is what I had signed up for, so I dealt with it, mostly turning to God in prayer.

For a few days I continued writing a letter I had started for them the night before they left. This helped to distract me from worrying about the girls' well-being. With tears streaming down my cheeks, it allowed me to grieve the loss of them from our family. I couldn't do anything about the current situation but I wanted to have something on paper to share with them one day if they ever came back. I wanted them to know that they were and still are loved so very much. I poured my heart out to them as I described the milestones they achieved, and what a huge blessing the past six months were, caring for them every moment of every day. I ended the letter with:

> *Papa and I are going to miss seeing your beautiful smiling faces every morning. It has been such a joy and a blessing to watch you beautiful girls grow and learn. I enjoyed doing everything for you each day because it allowed me to get to know you a little more, to love you a little more, to be your mama each day. My wish for you is that you will know love, safety, and happiness every day of your life.*
>
> *Love,*
> *Mama*

The moments I was privileged to experience with them are engraved in my memory and afforded me the chance to be mama to twin girls. My heart will always have a special place for them.

The boys and my husband and I were starting to get into a new routine. We appreciated the time we had to do things with just the boys, more so than before. I still wrestled with God about continuing down this fost-adopt path. The mental arguments with Him went something like, "I just want to enjoy the peaceful home life we have. I want to walk away from this adoption thing. It's too hard. Maybe this was all just another one of my not-so-great ideas that I forced upon my family. I just want to be comfortable with my life now, Lord." Really, what I was feeling and hoping to avoid was the risk of heartbreak. Then, like a movie that has been put on pause, the whirlwind of thoughts going through my mind came to an abrupt stop. I suddenly realized that none of this adoption, family building thing was really my doing. God had orchestrated the events thus far, not Elizabeth.

A couple of weeks after the twins were gone, another foster mom was in dire need of respite care (due to medical issues) for a new placement. When no one else volunteered, feeling badly for the fellow foster mom, I offered to take her placement for a couple of nights. A precious little blonde-haired, blue-eyed girl just over three years of age was brought to our house. The door of my husband's heart fell open no problem. Mine was guarded. "I won't have her long enough to know her, much less love her," were my initial thoughts. Thankfully, that is not how we were created to be no matter how badly we hurt. At some point our humanity takes over and our thinking shifts to the greater need. For a second my heart forgot about its pain and I saw her as God the Father saw her: a vulnerable child in need of a safe place to seek refuge.

Her small world had taken her for granted and treated her as though she was worthless, leaving her bruises as proof. My heart could not ignore the desperate need, no matter how badly it ached. It was not to be, though.

The foster mom was not going to be able to keep her due to some medical issues, and was I interested in taking her? I was torn. I didn't even know if my heart was ready to love and possibly lose another child. Was this God's will? What if the twins ended up back in the system? My friend was the voice of truth and reason, yet again, with words that every foster mom seeking to adopt should hear: "What if this is your forever daughter?" Essentially what my friend was challenging me to do was to just be willing to walk through the door. God, in His faithfulness, would lead me through to the other side if this was His will. We decided that if this precious baby girl needed a home to be kept safe and protected, if even just for a little while, or forever, then we would do it despite the cost to my heart. The day after we had decided we would have her (if they called us for placement), we found out that her former foster mom wanted to take her. God was faithful in leading us, but we had to be willing to sincerely walk through the doorway in faith.

Then, *the* call came.

Elizabeth Molina

16
The Call

About two weeks had passed since the twins had been reunified with their birth parents, and it was about two weeks before my trip to Hawaii. We had started to reacquaint ourselves with the idea of being a family of four but it somehow didn't feel right to any of us. Grant would walk into the twins' room and comment on how empty it felt. Jordan had come into his role as the oldest, the one I depended on for almost everything when Mario was working. He seemed to be at a loss of what to do with all his free time and was slightly confused with his position in the family. One day he had to be the responsible older brother pushing a stroller and helping to carry babies around and the next day he got to regress to the egotistical ways of a child. Mario enjoyed coming home and being able to relax but every other comment from him was, "I wonder how the girls are?" or that he missed them. It was really fun to watch him be a father to little girls. If God had said to my heart, "This is it, Elizabeth. This is the family I have for you," I would have been content. I would have felt peace in my heart. I know my God and how He speaks to me. I knew deep down He wasn't done with our family yet.

Our agency called. Were we interested in a 12-month-old and a 3-year-old sister sibling set? Their case was different than the norm. It was a bypass case, meaning that the birth parents were not offered rehabilitative services by the court. This can be for a variety of reasons. The court may choose to do this if it has terminated parental rights with another sibling, if the biological parents are unable to show a change in their circumstances, or if a truly heinous crime has been committed including the death of a child, abuse of a child under the age of five years, or severe physical or sexual abuse. The assigned social worker will make the recommendation to the court, but ultimately it is the court's decision to bypass services and to proceed with a more permanent plan.

These sisters had been in a foster home for the last eight months. It was time for the courts to decide if they were going to terminate parental rights and move toward a permanent plan for the girls. The way the system works is that if there are no potential adoptive parents identified, they can't terminate the birth parents' rights. Understandably, they won't create orphans. The problem was that the social worker had assumed that their then current foster parents were possible adoptive parents. Some people selflessly choose to provide a safe, caring environment for vulnerable children until they are either reunified or adopted. When it was brought to the social worker's attention that the current foster parents were not seeking to adopt, they had to identify a fost-adopt family quickly. The girls would then have to be in that placement for a minimum of six months before the social worker could recommend termination of parental rights.

At this point, my husband and I had agreed that we would continue on the fost-adopt path unless God pointed us in a different direction. As we contemplated our decision to take the placement, the wise words of my friend ran through my head again, over and over, "What if they are your forever daughters?" This case was exactly what I prayed for. It was as though God knew I couldn't handle heartbreak again. We met with social workers that week and heard the case history. This time, ever more consciously aware that God had His best in mind for us (and for them), we didn't hesitate. As soon as they asked us if we were interested in meeting them, we agreed without pause and in my heart I knew these would be my forever daughters!

As we waited for our first meeting with the girls, I remember sitting in the waiting room in the county building for what seemed like an eternity, feeling nervous and with my heart beating a mile a minute. Then I heard this tiny, squeaky, precious, little girl's voice in the stairwell. My heart melted. Could that be the voice of my forever daughter?

A while later we were ushered into a playroom where I saw the beautiful face that matched the precious voice I had just heard moments before. The older one, who liked to call herself Kitty, was a very busy three year old! She was cooking on a play kitchen stove, moving her hands as fast as she was talking and explaining everything she was doing to anyone who would listen. Then there was a shy, quiet, plump 12-month-old baby (nicknamed Itsy Bitsy by her foster parents), who was practicing standing and walking around slowly as she grasped the furniture. It was love at first sight!

I sat on a chair in the room and watched these two beautiful little girls, mesmerized. Their beauty was captivating. Kitty had big beautiful brown eyes, shoulder-length, straight brown hair, and the cutest pair of dimples that made me squeal inside every time she flashed them. The baby had short sandy brown hair that was still baby fine. Her big, brown eyes with long lashes emphasized the drama that her shyness brought out. She also had a set of dimples that I caught a sneak preview of that afternoon. Both appeared oblivious to the group of adults all watching as a family was forming before their eyes. It was as though all of us knew that something special was happening.

I still went to Hawaii but we had another visit planned with the girls before I left. We met with the foster mom at a beach park and she went to run errands while we played there with the girls. The baby was mostly reserved (and still not quite yet walking) and the precocious three year old was busy as ever. We brought some toys with us which the baby calmly enjoyed while the older sister wanted to climb, slide, and swing. I told her I would be going on a trip but I promised to bring her a necklace. Little did I know she had the memory of an elephant!

One of the biggest things advocated in foster care is self-care. As women, we sometimes think and act as though we are some sort of super human creature with the ability to handle everything in our life. It's true, we are very strong. God created us with the purpose of holding our families together and being a support for our husbands. Rest was also God's design, and who was I to argue about the way it was gifted to me. The trip to Hawaii was relaxing and allowed time for my mind and body to be renewed. While many biological families have similar or even more serious issues to deal with, foster families have normal age-related issues, issues relating to their specific case and then their own issues of bonding and attachment, as well as issues that come up when family dynamics are abruptly changed. So taking breaks and treating yourself to time-outs is high on the priority list. A trip to Hawaii, I felt, was completely justified and welcomed.

Mario and the boys had a visit with the girls while I was gone. They met up with the foster family at Chick-fil-A for lunch and play. This was their first time meeting the boys. According to my husband, Jordan and Grant fell seamlessly back into their roles as the older brothers. Kitty seemed excited to meet and play with the boys. They got along well. Even if they hadn't we would still have pursued the adoption because as the saying goes, "You get to choose your friends, not your family." This was true even for us, a family brought together through adoption. For all of us, biological, blended, or adopted it is not always perfect in our eyes but it surely is in the eyes of our Creator. He's always known how He was going to weave our family together.

I spoke with Kitty on the phone while they were all at Chick-fil-A. She reminded me that I had promised to bring her a necklace from Hawaii. I was on a mission. I couldn't disappoint! This necklace was more than just a souvenir of my trip. The fact that she remembered it each time I spoke with her placed a heavier weight on its significance. It was the first connection we had. I picked out a cute little Hello Kitty necklace at the Sanrio store at the mall while in Hawaii. Since she had nicknamed herself Kitty, I thought it would be a fitting choice.

When I came home from my trip, we arranged an afterschool visit at the foster parents' house. While on the phone confirming the time with the foster mom she said, "Kitty keeps mentioning this necklace you were going to bring her but if you didn't remember, that's ok." I assured the foster mom that I had made that my mission while in Hawaii. Secretly, I was thrilled that she remembered because that meant she remembered me! And so on that first visit she promptly reminded me of a necklace I promised her. I eagerly handed it over for her to examine and then carefully placed it around her neck. Her beaming smile and immediate hug told me it was a good choice.

Soon after that, we began overnight visits. The foster mom asked Kitty if she would like to have a sleepover at Miss Elizabeth's house. These visits were to ease the girls into the idea of yet another new home environment. We didn't flat out tell her it was going to be their new home. We began setting up the room for them little by little. When they came for their visit Kitty asked, "Whose beautiful room is this?" I told her, "It's for you and your sister whenever you want to visit." I am fully aware that a new room with new things is certainly not going to replace their loss, twice over. It does help them to plant new roots, gain a sense of comfort, and to imagine themselves in the new place for the long term.

Three homes and three sets of parents in three years is a lot to ask of a 3-year-old child. Add to that the trauma that had originally brought them into the system. While the baby seemed content as long as her basic needs were met, Kitty was having to process as much as her little mind could comprehend in a matter of weeks. The baby was still nonverbal but I don't think even Kitty could have voiced her feelings. The uncertainty of who "her family" was manifested in some difficult behaviors in those early days, but her ability to overcome what she has in her short life often still leaves me in awe of her!

Many people believe (and I was one of them prior to starting this adoption journey) that as long as you give a child food, shelter, safety, and love, they will be thankful, appreciative, and loving children. That is not always the case. Some kids just don't know how to attach, some associate it with pain, some are afraid of being hurt again, and some dislike expressing or receiving love or affection at all, as in the case of my oldest son. This inability to bond is not something expected to happen with a newborn or young infant unless there is a failure by the mother to meet the basic needs of the child. Even then, however, if another caregiver begins to meet those needs, the infant will most likely bond and attach easily to the new caregiver, which was the case for the baby. Unfortunately, the older the child is, the more she is aware of the change in caregivers. She also becomes more relational and begins to develop a sense of who she can trust. Although she may know how to bond, she may choose not to because of the high risk. Her behaviors may exhibit the opposite extreme of the spectrum. She may be indiscriminately affectionate with everyone, even strangers or visitors she has only just met that pay her the slightest bit of attention, but is not attached to any one person. This was the case with Kitty.

By the middle of May of 2014 the girls had transitioned full time from their former foster home to ours. Mario and I thought it would be better to limit the time the girls spent with their former foster family. We wanted the girls to see us as their primary caregivers. In essence, we were trying to rush the attachment process. We naively thought, *The sooner they detach from them, the sooner they will attach to us.* Once again, God reminded me that this adoption thing was not about me, but about these precious children that He loves so very much and for whom He wants the very best. It is certainly not a requirement to maintain the relationship with the former foster family but my friend's words rang true: The bonds of love are not meant to be broken and we certainly don't want our adopted or foster kids to learn this, inadvertently, in the process. We learned that broken attachments can adversely affect kids.

I am thankful that I did not sever those bonds, for my daughters' sake and my own. As I came to know their former foster mom more and more, she shared with me what she knew about our girls' case as well as the state in which the girls had come to them. It was heartbreaking to hear, but I will be forever thankful to her for caring, loving, and helping to heal our daughters. This drew us closer and she has now become Aunty Naw to our girls. They are always so excited to see her. Only she will fully know and completely comprehend the odds they had to overcome as she took them into her home and heart when they were most vulnerable. The bond created in that is one I am not willing to break.

17
Fake It 'til You Make It

After the honeymoon period ended, the transition got a bit rough. Kitty had been attending a preschool full time clear across the other side of town which was not conducive to our schedule. So we decided to pull her from that one and put her part time in a preschool up the street from our house. She attended Mondays and Wednesdays from 8:30 until 12:00. The baby stayed home with the boys and I, as I was still homeschooling them. The baby was on a schedule that allowed me to do some school work with them, but they were having to do more of it independently. I would run off and pick up Kitty from school, give the girls lunch, and then put the baby down for a nap. Kitty tried, but she just couldn't sleep. My oldest son never napped much either. But it was a struggle as Kitty couldn't seem to self-entertain even for just 20 minutes. Needless to say I started to get worn down.

Since we only did review work for school to keep the boys in practice, the summer was slightly easier to handle. The baby wasn't quite at the age where she could interact or play well with Kitty. The boys, on the other hand, would play well with Kitty but only for periods of time throughout the day. Mostly, it was up to me to entertain her. Add to that my other duties of being a stay-at-home mom, and it was exhausting. I thought this was what it was like for all mothers of four. After checking in with other moms, I realized it *was* a juggling act for all of us, but also taking time for oneself was equally important. It was at this time the necessity of regular self-care was reinforced. Yet I wasn't sure how to fit it in.

By early fall when school started up again, my patience was wearing thin; I was feeling ragged and I had completely neglected myself, pouring my all into my four kids. This was a recipe for disaster. I was starting to dislike ALL of my kids. Every little complaint, whine, and act of disobedience became another nail scratching the chalkboard. My social worker recommended a program that provided support for foster and adoptive families. This non-profit organization was a resource center that offered education and counseling services. It was for foster families in the trenches struggling to make sense of the craziness we experience daily with children that come from hard places. The counselor recommended that I take their course on Family Attachment.

While it was true that the kids and I needed help attaching, she soon realized I had no energy to even try because I was barely getting through each day. I learned many things in those 18 weeks including what self-care looks like, my own attachment style, and how my own upbringing affected how I related to each of the kids. That was a huge eye opener for me! Because I was raised in an atmosphere of constant fear and anxiety, I tended to discipline in that way. I yelled a lot, especially when I was overwhelmed and frustrated and tired; I demanded obedience out of fear and often resorted to ultimatums and threats that involved punishments that didn't fit the crimes. Especially for a child coming from trauma, but really for any child, it is not the best way to discipline. I am thankful that the counselor helped me to identify appropriate methods which included playfulness and do-overs. This lowered our anxiety and, at the same time, made the children feel safe.

Since then, I have read up on disciplining children that come from hard places. In Dr. Karyn Purvis' book, *The Connected Child*, she invites the parent to think in a new way about discipline because the "old way doesn't work" with children that have experienced trauma. "Rather than relying on traditional disciplinary techniques, you need an approach that combines firmness, kindness, and retraining."[1] Another nugget of wisdom I picked up somewhere is to Q-TIP: quit taking it personally. Harder said than done, for sure! But as I get older (and hopefully wiser), I feel like it is a little easier to not let the sass, aggression, eye-rolling, and the rude comments muttered under the breath affect me emotionally. I try to not even entertain them and just head straight to the issue at hand. I know they are meant to push my buttons and they just distract from the actual problem. I am certainly not proclaiming perfection in the parenting game, but I can attest to these tried and true methods.

Most probably the single best piece of advice the counselor gave me was to "fake it 'til you make it"; in other words, choose to show love, affection, and understanding every moment of each day—even if you don't feel it initially, but trusting yourself to adapt—because it's what the child needs. Sometimes it does feel like you are just babysitting someone else's kid. You remind yourself, if she had been yours from the beginning and hadn't experienced the things she did, she might behave differently. By redirecting the focus to what she has experienced, empathy sets in. Over time, you develop those deep feelings of love for her.

"Today I was hit, scratched, slapped, and screamed at by my 3-year-old foster daughter." I wrote this on the closed Facebook group for foster parents. She obviously didn't know how to deal with her feelings when frustration overcame her. Many three year olds don't. Just as with my boys, though, I could see the trauma behind her actions. My biggest concern was how to help her work through the pain and confusion she was dealing with. I asked the group of foster parents to please lift her precious little heart, mind, and body in prayer. I am sure at the time I wrote the post I was looking for a bit of sympathy, but more so, empathy from others who truly understood. I'm glad I wrote it. I'm able to look back on that difficult time and see how far my daughter has come.

By early fall I realized I needed to put Kitty back in preschool full time. Initially, I didn't want to because I felt the time spent together would be good for us and would help us with the attachment issues. Despite the financial cost and emotional toll it took on both of us, it was the best thing for her. She played all day, was engaged and mentally stimulated. When I picked her up, I tried to make the most of the time spent with her during the evening routine of dinner, bath, and bed. She usually fell asleep from sheer exhaustion within a minute of her head hitting the pillow. A bit of relief came from that decision to return her to preschool full time, but there were still issues to deal with.

There seemed to be a constant flow of notes coming home from preschool; one to two notes per week on average. It seemed excessive, but obviously warranted. I was appreciative of the communication and records of incidents for sure. There was the occasional potty accident but mostly she was either getting hurt or making a bad choice with other kids. As the symptoms of reactive attachment disorder (RAD) are described, Kitty was an overly active kid often taking risks which were meant to keep me (and other adults) constantly vigilant of her. This was consistent with the other RAD symptoms she was regularly displaying: she was a textbook example of RAD in her inability to self-entertain, her indiscriminate affections with anybody and everybody, and her need to constantly be busy doing things.[2]

Up to this point both girls were having weekly visits with their birth parent. Those mornings were particularly difficult. In the foster care world, birth parents are sometimes known as "Disneyland parents." Because they only have one hour a week with their kids, they come in with a whole slew of new toys, new clothes, and anything else they think their children want. It's like a day at Disneyland. My girls' birth parents were no exception. This happened EVERY week! I understood that this was their way of expressing love to their kids, but it was a bit excessive. It was getting harder and harder to keep up with them. I tried to be extra understanding on those days if the girls were overly emotional. I can't imagine what confusing thoughts were swirling around in their little brains.

In December of 2014, a court date was finally set. Eight months after being placed with us, parental rights were terminated. The very next day was their weekly visit with birth parents. It was their last visit, the goodbye visit—the one where the birth parents say goodbye but can't really say that they may never see them again, and the girls really didn't know that it would be their last time seeing their birth parents. Although I was thankful we were moving in the direction of permanency and stability for my girls, I still understood what this meant for their little hearts in whatever capacity it comprehended. I prayed for my girls that morning, that they would come to understand it all one day.

And I prayed for their birth parents. Another bittersweet day: As our family came together another family fell apart. My heart broke for the birth parents and for my girls' loss, although the removal from their parents was certainly warranted. I thought about what would have become of our girls had the system not stepped in on their behalf. Although it is not a perfect system, it is designed to protect those who can't protect themselves. We held our breath thinking that there would be an appeal but, thankfully, it never materialized.

The rest of the school year seemed to go a bit smoother as the girls settled into their roles in the family. We were still seeing behavioral issues with Kitty and again reached out to Kids & Families to help her work through it. They sent a therapist to our home once a week to conduct play therapy with her. This was extremely beneficial as she learned to appropriately deal with anxiety, identify and verbalize her feelings, and utilize the coping skills she learned. She started to show less oppositional behavior. This therapy was helpful for me, too! I learned to build a more secure attachment with her by using playfulness and empathy when correcting her misbehavior.

It wasn't perfect after that, but I had a renewed hope in my abilities to adapt to her. I did have to employ the "fake it 'til you make it technique" for a while. I was also sure to build some "me" time into the weekly schedule, which was a tremendous help dealing with four kids from hard places.

18
Love Story Complete

Eleven months later after parental rights had been terminated, the adoption of our little girls was finalized! We gave them new names–Hope (Kitty) and Laura (the baby). That morning, as I physically prepared everyone for the day's activities, I mentally mulled over the significance of the day. It struck me that after court that day, when I introduced my girls as my daughters, it would be legally true and a permanent reality! I recognized at that moment the overwhelming love in my heart for them that had grown over their time with us, despite our struggles. And this caused tears to flow out of me as I ached in my heart contemplating all that I wanted for my daughters and their precious lives.

There were occasional issues that would throw me for a loop. In adoption training many situations are presented and at the time you can completely understand them, but then you forget until it smacks you in the forehead. In early December, as I was decorating the Christmas tree, Hope suddenly turned somber after I asked her not to touch certain fragile decorations. Initially I thought she was upset because she couldn't touch the breakable decorations. Then she broke out in tears. I hadn't been harsh with her. When I asked her why she was crying, she said she missed her biological mom. I'm glad she was able to verbalize her feelings. As I had learned in adoption training classes, the holidays are, for foster and adopted kids, intense and highly emotional times that can cause depression and grief. The cheery atmosphere and overabundance of material things can be overwhelming to a child. The memory of certain traditions or horrible experiences during holidays can all be triggers that manifest in meltdowns and misbehavior.

 In an effort to comfort her, I offered to show Hope a photo of her birth mother. She looked at the photo and immediately said, "That's not her." Sadly, the picture in her head, the way she had come to imagine her, didn't match the photo. This is common with adopted children. Sometimes the child might create a fantastical picture of the birth family because a nicer version of a hard reality may be easier to swallow. This also shows where the child is at in processing her life story. We have always been open with Hope about being adopted but have decided to wait until she is older to share the details with her.

Laura was growing quickly. She was off bottles, had started talking in phrases, and then potty training moved up to the top of the list. All three of the older ones had pretty much come to me potty trained, so this was a bit of a foreign concept to me. I had no clue how to even start. My aunt came for an extended visit and told me I needed to give her Gatorade, Skittles, big-girl panties, and a princess potty. She showed me what to do; then we tried getting Laura to do it. She sat there obliging us for an hour as we tried everything we could think of to keep her entertained as she sat on the royal throne. We were rewarded an hour later with an ounce of pee in the chamber pot. Then she put her pull-up diaper back on with an attitude that said "Thanks for the Skittles, suckers," and was off to play, never giving the $30 princess potty a second look. She decided six months later that she didn't like the wet and mushy feeling of a dirty diaper anymore and one day just sat on the regular toilet.

It has really been interesting to watch as the kids take on some of our personality. When you have kids and you see those good and bad aspects of yourself in them, you just hope and pray that more of the good parts of you come through than the bad. You see them acting just like a mini you and at times you dread that reflection of yourself. You even try to change them. Recently I read that our weaknesses are our strengths misused. I think it's true.

Jordan is reserved, but has a dry sense of humor. He is quick-witted in a sly, quiet kind of way. Many times he has caught me off guard with his humorous responses while keeping a straight face and sends me reeling with laughter. Sometimes he knows exactly what to say to pull my heart strings. Recently, he was trying to explain why he ran the dog around the block instead of walking. We knew it was because he didn't want to pick up after it did its business. But instead of admitting to that, he matter-of-factly responded with, "I know Mama gets worried about me being gone too long." He also tends to be quite argumentative with us, but sharp. One time he talked me into letting Grant put strawberries in his noodles because, he argued, "How do all great chefs come up with new food combinations?" I can see the gears in his head going a mile a minute. I pray that his strong will and resilience will serve him well in his future. Since he was young he has always loved to direct how he and his brother play. This quality has already transferred to strong leadership on the soccer field as he shines with every opportunity to have his ideas heard.

Grant is outgoing, polite, and loving with everyone he encounters. He will offer a sturdy handshake while introducing himself without my prompting, and will greet most familiar faces with a bear hug. If he is grouchy or frustrated he usually only shows it in the safety of our family home. Only when he is either tired or hungry or has had enough of Hope pushing his buttons do we see this rare side of him. He is very easy going; willing to try almost any game, activity, or food I make with a positive attitude; and always has a smile on his face. He offers every guest something to drink when they enter our home and makes sure their comfort is foremost. He is very creative with his storytelling and loves to make things with his hands. There was a period of time when he was into making bows and arrows every day. If your birthday was approaching, he was sure that that was the perfect gift for you. He is very athletic and has a passion for basketball. The first week he was home he picked up a basketball and began dribbling it. At just four years old he was the youngest on my Upward basketball team.

Hope is sharp, energetic, creative, and inquisitive, but can be bossy. I remind her that she'll have her chance to direct others later in life. She knows exactly what she likes and doesn't like when it comes to style and has a fashion sense all her own. She loves to point out the obvious to her older brothers and tries to challenge them with useless trivia. She is also very loving and wants to make others feel special. She likes to make notes in her limited writing and decorate papers with stickers. She then rolls them up and seals them with old address labels if she can't find the box of envelopes I've hidden. Then she packs them into her backpack, climbs on her bike, and pedals down the street to deliver them to all the neighbors. She is not content to sit and play with dolls for longer than five minutes but she thrives on one-to-one attention and will sit and talk for hours with anyone who will listen to her. She is fearless and taught herself to ride a bike, a scooter, a skateboard, and skates.

Laura is quick-witted and will do almost anything to gain a laugh out of us, yet she is also strong-willed. Her tenacity is to be admired. Once she went almost a day without eating because she didn't like anything I offered her. She is more cautious than Hope with people she doesn't know well, but is lots of fun once she warms up to people. She is intent in her focus and will sit for 15 minutes on the driveway watching the meanderings of a roly poly. She is full of confidence and has informed me that she is ready for school. She thrives on the affections of her daddy and will cuddle up with me after her nap.

Our kids do not resemble us. At 14 and 11 years of age, our handsome boys are towering above us and are already stronger and faster than us. The girls are beautiful with light brown hair, olive colored skin, and dimples that are the first thing people notice about them. Because we have grown so comfortable with each other we forget that we stand out to people who don't know our story. Walking through the grocery store or sitting together in a restaurant I am reminded of this fact. I might notice someone staring at us or smiling at us. At first I think, maybe they are someone I know but can't place. But then I realize that their unusually long stare is almost begging to ask us the question, *How do we fit together?* I try to be considerate of my kids' feelings about discussing their adoption story with others. It is just that—their story. But in some ways it is also our family story. The sensitive details of their story I will leave to them to share if they choose to later in life. But I can't deny God's role in our family story. And without God, we would not have a story to tell.

In our family we deal with the same normal sibling rivalry that my husband and I experienced growing up. The boys are constantly wrestling, boxing, and competing with each other, but they are the best of friends and are often bored without the other. The girls bicker and fight with each other nonstop. After going an extended period of time without seeing each other, however, they are always so happy to be reunited. I am sure they will be the best of friends. The boys are the older brothers. They love their sisters and are constantly vigilant, ensuring their safety always. The girls look up to their brothers and enjoy being entertained by them.

I don't know that the boys would be as caring and loving without the girls in the picture. They are learning that the girls are more delicate and sensitive and are in need of their protection. And they step up in their role. Recently at the grocery store there was a young man wearing a t-shirt with inappropriate wording and pictures. I was busy picking out produce and hadn't noticed. Grant whispered quietly in my ear that he was going to walk his sister to another area within my line of sight so that she would not be exposed. Another time I had asked Grant to use a special cleaner for the toilet as he took his turn cleaning the bathroom. The youngest walked into the restroom wanting to wash her hands. He quickly escorted her out explaining that the fumes were too strong for her. Jordan is quick to carry Laura or grab Hope's hand when we are crossing a busy parking lot and has learned to help them settle their girly squabbles with love and kindness. Grant has been true to his word and has taught his little sisters many things. Recently Hope told me that Grant helped her make a chart to keep track of how often our beloved Chihuahua, Nanea, poops and pees every day. I'm not sure what the purpose of it was but she seemed appreciative of his help.

    Some people think they could never love an adopted child the same as a biological one. Although blood ties are important and are a strong part of a child's identity, they do not dictate the amount of love dealt to a child. Our hearts and minds do that. I was naive, that day in Haiti, to think that there wasn't enough room in my heart for anyone more than Jordan. Many a night, as they lie in bed about to close their eyes I ask them, "Do you know how loved you are? Do you know how precious you are to me? To God?" When I contemplate how much love God has given me for them and how deep that love runs, my heart is overwhelmed. I feel so utterly privileged to be their mom and am so completely smitten with each one of them.

I know God purposely led us to Haiti and also moved my heart at Adoption Story Night. Some days I just stop and stare at my kids in awe of God's plan for our family. I think about the way he has bound my heart so to theirs, and it brings me to tears. Francis Chan writes in his book, *Crazy Love*, "I came to understand that my desire for my children is only a faint echo of God's great love for me and for every person He made."[1] Through this adoption journey, I have learned to love like Jesus asks us to. Not every day. Not every moment. Not ever perfectly. But I strive to love like Jesus. I now understand what He meant when he said, "If I give all I possess to the poor and give over my body to hardship that I may boast, but do not have love, I gain nothing" (1 Corinthians 13:3; NIV). God measures our life by how well we have loved during our time here on this earth. That is how He loves us and how He desires us to love.

In his sermon titled *Adoption: The Heart of the Gospel*, John Piper draws the comparison of the earthly adoption to that of our spiritual adoption. Among the similarities he outlines are the fact that they were and are costly. "When people embrace the pain and joy of children..., the worth of Christ shines more visible."[2] Loving children that come with much trauma in their personal narrative is not easy and the emotional cost is great. But the joy of living in God's will completely overshadows the struggle. James said to "Consider it pure joy... whenever you face trials..." and "Blessed is the one who perseveres under trial because, having stood the test, that person will receive the crown of life that the Lord has promised to those who love him" (James 1:2,12, NIV).

Just as God knew that Jordan and Grant would become part of our forever family, He also knew that Hope and Laura would become our forever daughters. In His perfection, He orchestrated the coming together of our hearts and lives. Like the pieces of a puzzle, so He weaved the pieces of my heart to complete this love story.

Afterword

It's been two years since I began writing down our story. A lot has changed in that time. The twins were adopted by their grandmother. She also chose to not break those early bonds and we are privileged to see them on a regular basis. We have the pleasure of watching them grow as we continue to love them.

The boys are about to finish up their first year back in traditional school. Hope will be completing first grade and Laura, no longer a baby, finally got her wish to go to school like all the big kids. These kids amaze me every day in how they continue to adapt. Their resilience is impressive. There are still daily struggles but, when considering the big picture, I know they will all be just fine.

In the nine years that the boys have been with us, there is not a day that goes by that I don't think about the choice that their birth parents made. I will be forever grateful for the privilege of raising their boys. Recently, we were able to make contact with their birth family. We were all so happy to know they are alive and have survived the many natural disasters Haiti has withstood since 2009. A contentedness in their hearts was evidenced in the huge smiles on my sons' faces after we received photos and videos of their birth family. More than ever, we are determined to help Haiti however God leads us, now and when the boys are adults. Looking back, years down the road from that first day in November when I set foot on Haitian soil, I see that God had it all perfectly planned out, even when I couldn't see the perfection of His ways. He sowed in me seeds of love for this country and for the Haitian people in the deep recesses of my heart all those years ago.

 A few summers ago, my Pastor asked me to represent the mission component of our Vacation Bible School (VBS) at church. I had to rearrange our vacation plans to fit it in. I did so happily, as it would give me the opportunity to donate the offerings for the week to Chances for Children. This organization that orchestrated the adoption of my sons is very dear to me as it continues to work in the lives of many Haitians. Also, I had been asking the Lord to provide me with an opportunity to share about the work they are doing as well as the chance to raise funds for their programs in Haiti. I went into the week of VBS unsure as to what results it would produce. By the end of the week, I was so excited to have been a part of God's plan and purpose for our little VBS and thrilled at the outpouring of compassion I was blessed to witness. The children that attended could hardly comprehend what it meant to go without basic needs. I was told that in years past they had brought in offerings totaling $300, maybe $400 at most. By the end of VBS Sunday, offerings totaling over $750 had been given! I immediately emailed my friend Kathi at Chances for Children, thanking her for the opportunity to share in God's work caring for His people in Haiti. God could have used anyone to fill that gap in VBS but, in answering that call, I was tremendously blessed. It is truly amazing what the Lord can do through any of us if we are willing.

There are a number of ways to answer God's call to "Defend the weak and the fatherless; uphold the cause of the poor and the oppressed" (Psalm 82:3, NIV). I understand that not everyone feels called to adopt. There are a million organizations working in Haiti and just as many in the US that work with supporting foster kids and families. I feel it is of good stewardship to research and know well the organizations in which we invest our time and resources. Chances for Children and Defending the Fatherless are the two I can vouch for. I know the directors personally and I see them living the gospel and loving well as they serve the children of Haiti and Ventura County, respectively. I encourage you to seek out the many opportunities to bless and be blessed through these organizations.

Loving well,

Elizabeth

Elizabeth Molina

Notes

Introduction

1. Clarkson, S. (2014). *Own your life: Living with deep intention, bold faith, and generous love* (p. 180). Carol Stream, IL: Tyndale Momentum.

2. Clarkson, S. (2014). *Own your life: Living with deep intention, bold faith, and generous love* (p. 181). Carol Stream, IL: Tyndale Momentum.

3. Clarkson, S. (2014). *Own your life: Living with deep intention, bold faith, and generous love* (p. 180). Carol Stream, IL: Tyndale Momentum.

4. Clarkson, S. (2014). *Own your life: Living with deep intention, bold faith, and generous love* (p. 187). Carol Stream, IL: Tyndale Momentum.

Chapter 3

1. Lee, J. R., Hanley, J., & Hopkins, V. (1999). *What your doctor may not tell you about premenopause: Balance your hormones and your life from thirty to fifty* (pp. 122–123). New York, NY: Warner Books.

Chapter 6

1. Kendell, A. (2006). *Simple Haitian Creole for adoptive families* (pp. 6, 7). Author.

Chapter 8

1. The World Bank. (2015, March 12). *Four things you need to know about education in Haiti.* Retrieved on July 22, 2017, from The World Bank website: http://www.worldbank.org/en/news/feature/2

015/03/12/four-things-you-need-to-know-about-education-in-haiti

2. ChartsBin Statistics Collector Team. (2011). Daily calorie intake per capita. Retrieved on July 29, 2017, from http://chartsbin.com/view/1150

Chapter 12

1. Dingle, S. (2015, January 20). Please don't say "all kids do that" to adoptive and foster families... [Web log post]. Retrieved on February 27, 2017, from https://church4everychild.org/2015/01/20/please-dont-say-all-kids-do-that-to-adoptive-and-foster-families/

2. Purvis, K. B., Cross, D. R., & Sunshine, W. L. (2007). *The connected child: Bring hope and*

healing to your adoptive family (p. 64). New York, NY: McGraw-Hill.

3. Gerard, J. (2006, January 1). Reactive attachment disorder in adoptees [Web log post]. Retrieved on July 22, 2017, from http://www.rainbowkids.com/adoption-stories/reactive-attachment-disorder-in-adoptees-513

Chapter 17

1. Purvis, K. B., Cross, D. R., & Sunshine, W. L. (2007). *The connected child: Bring hope and healing to your adoptive family* (pp. 91, 93). New York, NY: McGraw-Hill.

2. Advocates for Children in Therapy (n.d.). Reactive attachment disorder vs. attachment disorder. Retrieved on July 22, 2017, from

http://www.childrenintherapy.org/attachment disorder.html

Chapter 18

1. Chan, F. (with Yankoski, D.). (2013). *Crazy love: Overwhelmed by a relentless God* (p. 57). Colorado Springs, CO: David C. Cook.

2. Piper, J. (2007, February 10). *Adoption: The heart of the gospel*. Message presented at the MICAH Fund Adoption Enrichment Seminar, Minneapolis, MN. Transcript retrieved on July 29, 2017, from http://www.desiringgod.org/messages/adoption-the-heart-of-the-gospel

Elizabeth Molina

Organizations/Resources

Chances for Children
https://www.chances4children.org/

Adoption Learning Partners
http://www.adoptionlearningpartners.org/

International Child Foundation
http://childfound.org/

Defending the Fatherless
http://www.defendingthefatherless.net/

Kids and Families Together
http://www.kidsandfamilies.org/

Ventura County Foster Care Agency
http://fostervckids.org/

Made in the USA
San Bernardino, CA
10 June 2018